This collection of essays explores new avenues in the ongoing debate on miracles and sheds light on various theological and philosophical issues. Presented as a dialogue between Robert Larmer and other leading philosophers in the field, both sides of the issues are provocatively explored.

Questions of Miracle provides an original and comprehensive exploration of the philosophical issues surrounding miracles. It will be a valuable reference book and teaching tool for scholars and students of theology, religious studies, and philosophy.

ROBERT LARMER is professor of philosophy, University of New Brunswick.

D1526416

Questions of Miracle

EDITED BY

ROBERT A. LARMER

McGill-Queen's University Press
Montreal & Kingston • London • Buffalo

© McGill-Queen's University Press 1996
ISBN 0-7735-1416-3 (cloth)
ISBN 0-7735-1501-1 (paper)

Legal deposit third quarter 1996
Bibliothèque nationale du Québec

Printed in Canada on acid-free paper

McGill-Queen's University Press is grateful to the
Canada Council for support of its publishing
program.

Canadian Cataloguing in Publication Data

Main entry under title:
Questions of miracle
Includes bibliographical references and index.
ISBN 0-7735-1416-3 (bound) -
ISBN 0-7735-1501-1 (pbk.)
1. Miracles   I. Larmer, Robert A., 1954-

BT97.2.Q48 1996   210   C96-900320-X

The following articles are reprinted with the permission of the authors and the
journals in which the articles originally appeared.

Fred Wilson, "The Logic of Probabilities in Hume's Argument against Miracles,"
   Hume Studies 15, no. 2 (1989): 255–76.
Robert Larmer, "Miracles and the Laws of Nature," *Dialogue* 24, no. 2 (1985):
   225–35.
John Collier, "Against Miracles," *Dialogue* 24, no. 2 (1986): 349–52.
Robert Larmer, "Against 'Against Miracles,'" *Sophia* 27, no. 1 (1988): 20–5.
Neil MacGill, "Miracles and Conservation Laws," *Sophia* 31, nos. 1 and 2 (1992):
   79–87.
Robert Larmer, "Miracles and Conservation Laws: A Reply to Professor
   MacGill," *Sophia* 31, nos. 1 and 2 (1992): 89–95.
Robert Larmer, "Miracles and Criteria," *Sophia* 23, no. 1 (1984): 5–12.
David Basinger, "Miracles and Natural Explanations," *Sophia* 26, no. 3 (1987):
   22–6.
Robert Larmer, "Miracles and Natural Explanations: A Rejoinder," *Sophia* 28, no.
   3 (1989): 7–12.
David Basinger, "Miracles as Evidence for Theism: A Surrejoinder," *Sophia* 29, no.
   1 (1990): 56–9.
Robert Larmer, "Miracles, Evidence and Theism: A Further Apologia," *Sophia* 33,
   no. 1 (1994): 51–7.
Phillip Wiebe, "Authenticating Biblical Reports of Miracles," *Journal of Philosophical
   Research* 18 (1993): 309–25.
Christine Overall, "Miracles as Evidence against the Existence of God," *The
   Southern Journal of Philosophy* 22, no. 3 (1985): 347–53.

*To my wife Lorena Henry
thank you for all we share*

Contents

viii   Contents

Preface
Miracles: A Continuing Debate

ROBERT LARMER

I have brought together this collection of articles for two reasons. First, the ongoing debate over miracles is of great theoretical and practical significance. One cannot discuss miracles without very quickly being drawn into important issues concerning agency, causality, the relation of evidence to belief, conceptions of the laws of nature, the form of genuine explanations, and providence and God's operation in the world, to name only a few.

Second, although the topic is an important one, most work on miracles, at least in contemporary philosophy and theology, appears in the form of isolated journal articles. Such an approach has the advantage of encouraging the expression of a diversity of viewpoints, but it suffers the drawback of fostering a piecemeal approach to a complex issue. Unfortunately, extended and systematic treatments of the topic are few and far between.

Although I would argue that extended treatments are valuable – I have recently contributed a book on the topic[1] – such an approach does not so easily reflect philosophical diversity. The present collection is an attempt to develop a *via media* between these two approaches. The format I have chosen is that of a series of articles in which I engage in a dialogue with other philosophers on various issues associated with the topic of miracles. A consequence of selecting this format is that approximately half this collection consists of articles I have contributed myself. My defence of this imbalance is that it does not rest upon the demands of my ego but rather upon my desire to illustrate a comprehensive and unified approach in the midst of philosophical diversity. My aim has been not simply to depict the diversity of viewpoints with regard to miracles but rather to explore the resources of my position in dealing with a variety of opposing views.

Given this goal, it is appropriate to say something, however brief, about the history of critical debate on miracles. My remarks are meant only to set the stage for the discussion that takes place in the body of this book and to say something useful about what has gone before, in order to assess more accurately the contemporary debate. In no way should my remarks be understood as attempting a comprehensive treatment of a subject that requires a book in its own right.[2]

At least in Western philosophy, critical reflection on the topic of miracles begins with the rise of Christianity. That Jesus fulfilled the Old Testament prophecies of a coming Messiah and that his miracles are confirmation that in Him the Messiah has arrived was regarded by first- and second-century apologists as the strongest argument for Christianity. As F.F. Bruce comments, "In the proclamation of the apostles the argument from prophecy and the argument from miracle coincided and culminated in the resurrection of Jesus. This was the supreme messianic sign, the greatest demonstration of the power of God, and it was at the same time the conclusive fulfilment of those prophecies which pointed to the Messiah."[3]

Early apologists were aware that the evidential value of miracles could not reside simply in the fact that they are unusual events. Origen, who was prepared to say that without miracles the early Church could not have been established, did not define an event as a miracle solely on the basis that it was unusual.[4] In his view, the mighty works of Jesus are to be judged miracles not simply on the ground that they are dramatic exceptions to the usual course of nature but also by virtue of the fact that they fulfil Old Testament prophecies concerning the Messiah. Similarly, the miracles of the apostles and later Christians must be understood not just as exceptions to the usual course of nature but as furthering the transforming and healing work of the Church.

Somewhat later, we find Augustine, the most influential theologian of the early church, taking up the question of miracles and their relation to Christian faith. In his early writings, we find both important similarities and dissimilarities to the views of the early Fathers. Like earlier apologists, Augustine was prepared to say that miracles played an essential role in establishing Christianity, but unlike earlier apologists, he did not feel that miracles play a significant part in the ongoing work of the Church:

We have heard that our predecessors, at a stage in faith on the way from temporal things up to eternal things, followed visible miracles. They could do nothing else. And they did so in such a way that it should not be necessary for those who came after them. When the Catholic Church had been founded and diffused throughout the whole world, on the one hand miracles were not allowed to continue till our time, lest the mind should always seek visible things, and the human race should grow cold by becoming accustomed to things which when they were novelties kindled its faith. On the other hand we must not doubt that those are to be believed who proclaimed miracles which only a few had actually seen, and yet were able to persuade whole peoples to follow them. At that time the problem was to get people to believe before anyone was fit to reason about divine and invisible things.[5]

Augustine was later to retract his early view, and came to believe, both on the basis of testimony and personal experience, that miracles continue to occur and play an important part in the mission of the Church. In *The City of God* he remarks, "The truth is that even today miracles are being wrought in the name of Christ ... such miracles do not strike the imagination with the same flashing brilliance as the earlier miracles ... The fact that the canon of our Scripture is definitively closed brings it about that the original miracles are everywhere repeated and are fixed in peoples' memory, whereas contemporary miracles which happen here or there seldom become known even to the whole of the local population in and around the place where they occur."[6] He immediately follows this claim with an account of a miracle he personally witnessed. Elsewhere in *The City of God*, he chronicles his realization of "how many miracles ... [are] occurring in our own day and which [are] so like the miracles of old ... It is only two years ago that the keeping of records was begun here in Hippo, and already, at this writing, we have nearly seventy attested miracles. I know with certain knowledge of many others which have not, so far, been officially recorded."[7] Writing later in *The Retractions*, Augustine again stressed the continuing occurrence of miracles and their importance in the life of the Church.[8]

Aquinas, the most formative medieval philosopher and theologian, largely follows Augustine in his treatment of miracles. According to Aquinas, miracles understood in a strict sense are the province of God alone.[9] They are so because miracles, properly defined, are events beyond the ability of nature to produce.[10] If a created being brings about an event, however marvellous, the event is a natural one, since it lies within the natural powers of such a being to bring about events of that kind. Angels or demons may produce unusual events beyond the power of any human to duplicate, but these are not, properly speaking, miracles, for "when a finite power produces the proper effect to which it is limited, it is not a miracle although it may be wonderful to one who does not understand that power ... there is no miracle if an effect be produced by a higher cause by means of its proper principles. Therefore it is altogether impossible for miracles to be wrought by the power of ... higher creatures."[11] Since he emphasizes that miracles are entirely beyond the capabilities of nature, Aquinas insists that we cannot speculate on the manner in which miracles occur. Whereas Augustine was prepared to suggest that miracles might occur through the acceleration of natural processes, Aquinas' view was that miracles involve the direct action of God without the use of intermediate processes.

There is in Aquinas and the early Augustine a subtle, but significant, shift of emphasis. Earlier apologists such as Origen argued that miracles play an important role in establishing the truth of Christianity and furthering the ongoing mission of the Church. They did not think it necessary, however, to argue that the primary purpose of miracles was to validate theological truth-claims. In contrast, Aquinas and the early Augustine incorporate this further element into their arguments. Aquinas writes, "God works ... [miracles] for man's benefit, and this in two ways: in one way for the confirmation of the truth declared, in another way in proof of a person's holiness, which God desires to propose as an example of virtue. In the first way miracles can be wrought by any one who preaches the faith and calls upon Christ's name ... In the second way miracles are not wrought except by the saints, since it is in proof of their holiness that miracles are wrought during their lifetime or after death."[12]

This shift is important. In general, later discussions simply assume that the sole purpose of a miracle is to guarantee the truth of Christian doctrine. Thus a miracle such as Christ feeding the multitude is interpreted as Jesus making a claim that he is the Messiah. That this assumption creeps into the discussion is unfortunate on two counts. First, it leads to an interpretation that is at odds with the New Testament account of Christ's miracles.[13] Second, it ignores the apologetic richness of an understanding that sees miracle not simply as a guarantee of doctrine but as part of God's gracious response to human suffering.

The assumption that the purpose of a miracle is to guarantee the truth of doctrine manifests itself in the writings of the great reformers Martin Luther and John Calvin. Both expressed the view that the purpose of Christ's miracles was to establish that he is the Messiah, and both believed that the age of miracles was past. Given that the Canon was closed and the church established, miracles could serve no further purpose. In a passage reminiscent of the early Augustine, Luther writes that "now that the apostles have preached the Word and have given their writings, and nothing more than what they have written remains to be revealed, no new and special revelation or miracle is necessary ... miracles are no longer necessary ... [since] no further words of revelation are to be expected. In the beginning, when the young trees were still undeveloped and new, they had to be tied to a stake until they became strong. But now that the Word has been disseminated throughout the world, there is no longer any need to confirm it."[14]

If the primary purpose of miracles is conceived as guaranteeing doctrine, it becomes essential to deny that they could be performed through or by those holding incorrect views. In his "Prefatory Address to King Francis," Calvin both defends himself against the Catholic challenge that he can point to no miraculous confirmation of his doctrines and attacks the Catholic appeal to post-apostolic miracles.

In demanding miracles of us, they [Catholics] act dishonestly. For we are not forging some new gospel, but are retaining that very gospel whose truth all the miracles that Jesus Christ and his disciples ever wrought serve to confirm. But compared with us, they have a strange power: even to this day they can confirm their faith by continual miracles! Instead they allege miracles which can disturb a mind otherwise at rest – they are so foolish and ridiculous, so vain and false ...

Perhaps this false hue could have been more dazzling if Scripture had not warned us concerning the legitimate purpose and use of miracles. For Mark teaches that those signs which attended the apostles' preaching were set forth to confirm it (Mark 16:20) ... When we hear that they [miracles] were appointed only to seal the truth, shall we employ them to confirm falsehoods? In the first place, it is right to investigate and examine that doctrine which, as the Evangelist says, is superior to the miracles. Then, if it is approved, it may rightly be confirmed from miracles ... we may ... fitly remember that Satan has his miracles which, though they are deceitful tricks rather than true powers, are of such a sort as to mislead the simple-minded and untutored (cf. II Thess. 2:9–10). Magicians and enchanters have always been noted for miracles. Idolatry has been nourished by wonderful miracles, yet these are not sufficient to sanction for us the superstition either of magicians or of idolaters.

... [T]hose 'miracles' which our adversaries point to in their own support are sheer delusions of Satan, for they draw the people away from the true worship of their God to vanity (cf. Deut. 13:2ff.).[15]

Calvin's emphasis on the Christian Scriptures as the Word of God and his insistence that the individual's experience of the Holy Spirit witnessing through Scripture is the ultimate authority grounding doctrine and praxis provoked the development of the New Pyrrhonism by Roman Catholic apologists. Named after the early sceptic Pyrrho, this movement aimed to undermine any possibility of objective knowledge. Specifically, it denied the possibility of the individual believer knowing Scripture to be God's word or of being able to interpret it correctly. The hope was that, shorn of any pretence to knowledge, Protestants would return and acknowledge the authority of the Catholic faith.

As an apologetic strategy the New Pyrrhonism was ill-considered. It was not long before Protestant apologists redirected the sceptical arguments of the New Pyrrhonists against the Catholic church; denying that there is any reason to accept Rome's claim to truth or authority. The effect of the New Pyrrhonism was not to convert the Protestants, but to raise doubts about the possibility of knowledge. It is against this backdrop of uncertainty that the subsequent discussions of the seventeenth and early eighteenth centuries must be understood.

The development of European rationalism was, in many respects, a response to the climate of scepticism engendered by the New Pyrrhonism. The rationalists shared with the sceptics the view that knowledge must be beyond any possibility of doubt and that much of what has customarily been claimed as knowledge does not fall into this category. They aimed to refute scepticism by uncovering that which is beyond doubt.

A consequence of this scepticism and the rationalist reaction to it is that Christian apologists were no longer able to take for granted the historical reliability of the New Testament accounts of miracles. Spinoza cautions his readers that "in order to interpret the Scriptural miracles and understand from the narration of them how they really happened, it is necessary to know the opinions of those who first related them, and have recorded them for us in writing, and to distinguish such opinions from the actual impression made upon their senses, otherwise we shall confound opinions and judgments with the actual miracle as it really occurred: nay, further, we shall confound actual events with symbolical and imaginary ones. For many things are narrated in Scripture as real, which were in fact only symbolical and imaginary."[16] This shift of emphasis from the question of what is the evidential value of miracles to whether miracles, qua extraordinary events, can be established becomes a dominant feature of subsequent discussions.

Spinoza insists that even if extraordinary events can be established, all that can be meant in calling an event a miracle is that we are ignorant of its cause.[17] Given that we are sure that the laws of nature have no exceptions and that all events have natural causes,[18] it is clear that miracles can never function as evidence for the existence of God or confirmation of theological doctrine. In Spinoza's view, miracles are either products of the religious imagination or events for which we do not yet have an explanation. Although it is clear that his insistence that all events have natural causes and that to call an event a miracle is merely to baptise human ignorance is a consequence of his identifying God and nature, Spinoza again sounds a theme that becomes important in subsequent discussions.

Thomas Hobbes can scarcely be classified as a rationalist, but we find in his discussion of miracles much the same approach as Spinoza. Hobbes was too circumspect to deny outright the occurrence of the biblical miracles, but he did not hesitate to accept Calvin's claim that miracles no longer occur. His argument in support of this conclusion is essentially Spinoza's, namely that purported miracles are either the product of the religious imagination or poorly understood natural phenomena: "in these times I do not know one man that ever saw any such wondrous work, done by the charm or at the word or prayer of a man, that a man endued with but a mediocrity of reason would think supernatural: and the question is no more whether what wee see done, be a miracle; whether the miracle we hear, or read of, were a real work, and not the act of a tongue or pen; but in plain terms, whether the report be true or a lye."[19]

We find in Blaise Pascal, a contemporary of Spinoza and Hobbes, a very different approach to the question of miracles. Pascal, although he left no systematic outworking of his philosophy, seems to choose a *via media* between the scepticism of the New Pyrrhonists and the dogmatism of the rationalists. His view appears to be that consistent scepticism is impossible but that human reason cannot be autonomous, that is, it needs a ground outside itself. Reason is best grounded in the God of theism, but the mystery of God's existence and His creation of the universe take us far beyond the scope of reason. Lack of faith is unreasonable, but true religion can never be solely a matter of the intellect. It demands also a response of the heart, a faith in the living God whom reason can never wholly comprehend.

This general approach is mirrored in his treatment of the evidential value of miracles. It would be unreasonable to deny that

Christ's miracles and fulfilment of prophecy confirm that he is the Messiah, but any acceptance of Jesus as God must also involve an act of faith and a response to God's grace. Reason points to something beyond itself but cannot compel the further step of faith. Pascal's way of putting this is that Christ's miracles and fulfilment of prophecy provide "enough evidence to condemn and not enough to convince, so that it should be apparent that those who follow ... are prompted to do so by grace and not by reason, and those who evade ... are prompted by concupiscence and not by reason."[20]

A critic such as Spinoza might have been inclined to charge that Pascal is naive in thinking that events so obviously the product of religious imagination actually occurred as recorded. This criticism would not have overly bothered Pascal, since he did not subscribe to the Calvinist thesis that miracles no longer occur. On 23 March 1656, Pascal's niece, Marguerite Perrier was healed of a serious disfiguring lachrymal fistula in her eye; her healing was supported by substantial medical evidence and authenticated by diocesan authorities.[21] This healing was but one of a large number of Jansenist miracles that Pascal had personal knowledge of and accepted as genuine. Pascal could quite properly reply to Spinoza that once it has been established that similar events continue to occur, there is no reason to accept the hypothesis that the miracles recorded in the New Testament are figments of the religious imagination.

Pascal was not the only thinker of the period to seek a *via media* between the Scylla of scepticism and the Charybdis of rationalism. We find in the virtuosi of England's Royal Society, men such as Robert Boyle, Joseph Glanvill, and John Wilkins, a conscious attempt to steer a middle path between these two extremes.[22]

Characteristic of this approach was a rejection of the egocentric notion of knowledge employed by the sceptics and rationalists. These thinkers emphasized that the achievement of knowledge is a communal affair and hence that testimony can be a source of knowledge. Equally characteristic is their emphasis that moral, as opposed to absolute, certainty grounds human knowledge. Truth is to be apprehended through probability judgments of increasing adequacy. The ultimate presupposition of the epistemology of these men is the existence of God, who creates not only the natural objects studied but the human mind capable of scientific inquiry.[23]

These thinkers placed an emphasis on the apologetic value of miracles unparalleled except in the writings of the early Fathers. They appealed to miracles not as proving the existence of God but as confirming the revelation of God. Miracles are the proof that Christianity is God's authentic revelation. Thus Glanvill writes that "if there be a Providence that superviseth us, (as nothing is more certain) doubtless it will never suffer poor help-less creatures to be inevitably deceived by the craft and subtlety of their mischievous enemy, to their undoing; but will without question take such care, that the works done by Divine Power for the confirmation of Divine Truth, shall have such visible marks and signatures, if not in their nature, yet in their cir-cumstances, ends and designs as shall discover whence they are, and sufficiently distinguish them from all imposture and delusions."[24]

Miracles are not to be defined simply on the basis that they are unusual events. The context in which they occur and the character of the person by which, or through which, they are performed must be taken into account. Glanvill comments that it is not the strangeness, or unaccountableness of a thing ... from whence we are to conclude a miracle ... they have peculiar circumstances that speak them of a divine origin. Their mediate authors declare them to be so, and they are always persons of simplicity, truth and holiness, void of ambition, and all secular designs. They seldom use ceremonies, or natural applications, and yet surmount all the activities of known Nature. They work those wonders, not to raise admiration, or out of the vanity to be talked of; but to seal and confirm some Divine doctrine, or commission, in which the good and happiness of the world is concerned.[25]

These thinkers were aware that this appeal to the principle of context opened them to the charge of circular reasoning, in-asmuch as it could be objected that they established miracles on the basis of doctrine and doctrine on the basis of miracles. Their reply was that the question of whether an unusual event occurred must be distinguished from the question of whether it is a miracle. Whether or not the event occurred is not es-tablished on the basis of doctrine, but whether it is a genuine miracle is established on the basis of doctrine. Their argument seems to be that it is possible, on the basis of testimonial evidence, to establish the occurrence of an event that is an exception to the usual course of nature. Whether such an event is a miracle can then be decided on the basis of whether it is consistent with Christian doctrine, which, although it transcends natural religion, is in accordance with it. The event may then be seen as a confirmation of the revelatory elements in the doctrine that transcend unaided human reason. Boyle makes essentially this argument when he writes that

[since] supernatural things that are wont to be accounted miracles, may proceed from two extremely differing causes, namely God and the Devil, it is necessary to consider the nature of the doctrines for which miracles are vouched, that we may not perniciously mistake diabolical works for divine miracles. And if it be replied, that however by this way of proceeding we do not judge of a doctrine by the miracles that attest it, but we judge of the miracles by the doctrines whereunto it bears witness, I rejoin that the objection is grounded upon a mistake. For I do not think we should determine that this, or that, determinate matter of fact is to be asserted or denied upon the account of the doctrine it is employed to attest; nor yet, that a miracle, competently attested ought to have its authority rejected because it agrees not with this or that particular article of this or that particular religion. But I think that the use we ought to make of a doctrine in judging of a miracle is not to deny the historical part, if it be substantially attested, but to distinguish whether it be likely to come rather from some evil spirit than from God ... Yet I presume not to judge which of these two the miracle is by the articles of any particular instituted religion ... but for this examination take only the general principles of natural reason and religion, which teaching me antecedently to all particular revelations, that there is a God, that he is, and can be but one ... just, wise, good, gracious ... If a supernatural effect be wrought to authorize a doctrine yet plainly contradicts these truths, I cannot judge such a miracle to be divine ... But if the revelation backed by a miracle proposes nothing that contradicts any of these truths ... and much more if it proposes a religion that illustrates and confirms them; I then think myself obliged to admit both the miracle, and the religion it attests.

... Thus I first assent to a natural religion upon the score of natural

reason ... And then; if a miracle be wrought ... if I find by the agreea-
bleness of it to the best notions that natural theology gives us ... that
this religion cannot in reason be doubted to come from [God]; I then
judge the body of the religion to be true. And if anything yet is obscure
or doubtful in that religion, a miracle should be wrought to decide
the difficulty, I would submit to that decision, and not judge the miraculous matter of fact competently attested, to be false, 'cause it is
repugnant to some preconceived opinions of mine."[26]

The emphasis upon miracles as the foundation of revealed religion provoked a reaction on the part of the Deists, who were
concerned to undermine not belief in God but the rationality
of moving from natural theology to divine revelation. In the
main, their concern was to prove not that miracles could not
or did not occur, but that they could never serve to authenticate
revelation.

The Deists were especially anxious to turn the principle of
context against the virtuosi. They developed a number of a posteriori arguments to show that the evidence for the New Testament miracles is either dubious or nonexistent. One of their
favourites was that the virtuosi applied a double standard in accepting the miracles of Jesus but refusing to countenance the
miracles of medieval saints or rival religions. Thus Thomas
Chubb writes that "[t]he miracles wrought in, and by the Church
of Rome, for ages past, has been looked upon, and in general
treated by Protestants, as fraud and imposition; though it has
been wholly out of the power of those Protestants to prove some
of them to be such; and though some of these facts seem to
be better attested than any of the miracles which were wrought
or supposed to be wrought in the first century."[27]

This stock argument that the miracles of rival religions or de-
nominations cancel the evidential value of each other was later
picked up by David Hume in his essay "Of Miracles" and employed as his fourth a posteriori argument against miracles.[28]
In reading the Deists, it becomes clear that the arguments employed by Hume in part 2 of the essay are not his own invention,
but are commonplace in the philosophical literature of the time.[29]
It also becomes clear that Hume's famous a priori argument, developed in part 1 of the essay, that it is in principle impossible
to justify belief in a miracle on the basis of testimonial evidence,

was anticipated by earlier writers. Both Joseph Butler and Thomas Sherlock argue against a version of it, and both William Wollaston and Peter Annet employed versions of it.[30] Surprisingly, although we know that he was familiar with the writings of these men, Hume shows no awareness that this argument has a prior history and regards it as originating with himself.[31]

Contrary to the assertions of writers such as Antony Flew,[32] Hume's claim to fame as regards miracles lies not in initiating philosophical analysis nor in the originality of his arguments. It lies, rather, in the apparently clear and forceful way in which he put these arguments. I say "apparently clear and forceful" because many philosophers both then and now think that the initial impression of simplicity and elegance that marks the essay "Of Miracles" is deceptive. While it is possible to debate the merits of Hume's arguments, what cannot be denied is that his formulation of the arguments, especially the a priori argument of part 1 that no amount of testimonial evidence can justify belief in a miracle, has had an enormous influence on subsequent discussions of miracle.

We can discern in the historical debate two types of objections to belief in miracles. One type, associated with the rationalist tradition, focuses on the metaphysical impossibility of miracles: they are thought to be impossible either because there exists no transcendent Creator capable of overriding nature or because it would be inconsistent for God to work miracles. The second type, associated with the empiricist tradition, focuses on epistemological difficulties. The rationality of belief in miracles is thought to be difficult, perhaps impossible, to establish because of the difficulties in demonstrating the occurrence of miracles.

We find in the rise of theological liberalism that marked the nineteenth century a curious mingling of these two types of criticism. We find the epistemological arguments so characteristic of Hume, but even more fundamentally, we find metaphysical presuppositions reminiscent of Spinoza. The reason is not hard to fathom. Nineteenth-century liberals were greatly influenced by German idealism, and the German idealists, like Spinoza before them, identified God and nature. Given their metaphysics, miracles were logically impossible inasmuch as the identity of God and nature precludes any overriding of nature by a divine Creator. It is no accident that the paradigmatic exemplar of nineteenth-century liberalism, David Strauss, who was willing to talk of the identity of the human and Divine Spirit,[33] felt compelled to explain the Gospel miracles as products of the myth-making propensity of the early Church, insisting that "in the person and acts of Jesus no supernaturalism shall be suffered to remain."[34] Despite the liberals' familiarity with and use of the Deists' a posteriori arguments against miracles, there can be little doubt that the rise of "higher criticism" and the quest for the historical Jesus, that is, the non-miracle-working Jesus, were fundamentally the outworking of the liberals' metaphysical rejection of the possibility of miracle.

Just as Pascal provides a marked contrast to the rationalism of Spinoza, John Henry Newman provides a marked contrast to nineteenth-century liberals. Both Pascal and Newman insisted that although miracles have an evidential value, they must not be viewed as bare atomic events but rather as part of a larger system, and both men insisted that miracles did not cease with the apostolic age.

Newman replies to the charge that miracles are antecedently improbable because we can find no parallels to them in our personal experience by arguing that the probability of a miracle must be evaluated with regard not only to our experience of physical order but also to our experience of moral order. Given our experience of acting on the physical order to achieve or preserve moral order, a miracle "is very far indeed from improbable, when a great moral end cannot be effected except at the expense of physical irregularity."[36] Against those in the Reformed tradition who claim that miracles once occurred but no longer do, he argues that "miracles are not only not unlikely, they are positively likely ... it is incomparably more difficult to believe that the Divine Being should do one miracle and no more, than that He should do a thousand; that He should do one great miracle only, than that He should do a multitude of less besides."[37]

Ernst Troeltsch's famous paper "On Historical and Dogmatic Method in Theology," written at the close of the nineteenth century, marks a return to the epistemological concerns that have so marked the twentieth-century debate. Troeltsch argues that

analogy with what happens before our eyes and comes to pass in us is the key to criticism. Deception, dubious dealings, fabrication of myth, fraud and party spirit which we see before our eyes are the means by which we recognize the same kind of thing in the material which comes to us. Agreement with normal, ordinary, repeatedly attested modes of occurrence and conditions, as we know them, is the mark of probability for the occurrences which criticism can acknowledge as having really happened or leave aside. The observation of analogies between homogeneous occurrences of the past makes it possible to ascribe probability to them and to interpret what is unknown in the one by the known in the other.[38]

This is essentially the a priori argument developed by Hume in part 1 of the essay "Of Miracles" that since miracles have no parallel in our experience, reports of miracles must be rejected on the basis of antecedent improbability. It is always more likely that the reports are products of deception or credulity than that a miracle occurred, and it is therefore impossible to justify belief in miracles on the basis of testimonial evidence.

Brief though our historical survey has been, it makes clear that knowledge of the history of the debate is important if we are to evaluate the significance and worth of twentieth-century contributions. C.S. Lewis, commenting on the phenomenon of what he called "chronological snobbery," once noted the tendency towards "the uncritical acceptance of the intellectual climate common to our own age and the assumption that whatever has gone out of date is on that account discredited."[39] He goes on to say that "[y]ou must find why it went out of date. Was it ever refuted (and if so by whom, where, and how conclusively) or did it merely die away as fashions do?"[40]

The present volume will be successful if it encourages the reader to explore an important and interesting debate, not only as it exists in the twentieth century but as it has progressed and developed from the time of earliest Christianity.

NOTES

1 See my Water Into Wine? (Montreal: McGill-Queen's University Press 1988).
2 See, for example, Colin Brown, Miracles and the Critical Mind (Grand Rapids, MI: Eerdmans 1984); R.M. Burns, The Great Debate on Miracles

xxiv Preface

(London: Associated University Presses 1981); R.M. Grant, *Miracle and Natural Law in Graeco-Roman and Early Christian Thought* (Amsterdam: North Holland Publishing Co. 1952); C.F.D. Moule, ed., *Miracles: Cambridge Studies in their Philosophy and History* (London: Mowbrays 1965).

3 F.F. Bruce, *The Apostolic Defence of the Gospel*, 2d ed. (1967; reprint, London: Inter-Varsity Press 1970), 12.

4 Origen, *Against Celsus* 1.46., writes, "I shall refer not only to His [Jesus'] miracles, but, as is proper, to those also of the apostles of Jesus. For they could not without the help of miracles and wonders have prevailed on those who heard their new doctrines and new teachings to abandon their national usages, and to accept their instruction at the danger to themselves even of death. And there are still preserved among Christians traces of ... [the] Holy Spirit. They expel evil spirits, and perform many cures, and foresee certain events, according to the will of the Logos." *The Ante-Nicene Fathers*, ed. Alexander Roberts and James Donaldson (Edinburgh edition 1885; reprint Grand Rapids, MI: Eerdmans 1968), 4: 415.

5 Augustine *Of True Religion*, 47; quoted from J.H.S. Burleigh, ed., *Augustine: Earlier Writings*, The Library of Christian Classics, vol. 6 (Philadelphia: Westminster Press 1953), 48.

6 Augustine *City of God* 17–22, trans. Gerald G. Walsh, S.J. Honan, and Daniel J. Honan, in *The Fathers of the Church* (Washington DC: The Catholic University of America Press 1954) 24, bk. 22, chap. 8, 432–3.

7 *City of God* 22. 8.

8 Augustine *The Retractions*, trans. Sister Mary I. Bogan, in *The Fathers of the Church*, vol. 60 (Washington, DC: The Catholic University of America Press 1968). See, for example 1.12.7 and 1.13.5.

9 Aquinas *Summa Theologica* 114. 4; *Summa Contra Gentiles* 3. 102, in *See Basic Writings of Saint Thomas Aquinas*, ed. Anton C. Pegis (New York: Random House, 1945), 1: 1052; 2: 199–201.

10 *ST* 2–2. 105.7.

11 *SG* 3. 102.

12 *ST* 2–2. 178. 2. In Aquinas, *Summa Theologica*, trans. Fathers of the English Dominican Provence (New York: Benziger, 1947).

13 Most of Jesus' miracles seem a response to human suffering rather than an attempt to prove he is the Messiah. For example, Matthew (15:32) explicitly states that his reason for feeding the four thousand is his compassion for the hungry people.

14 Martin Luther, *Sermons on the Gospel of St. John*, Chaps. 14–16, in

Luther's Works, ed. Jaroslav Pelikan, vol. 24 (St Louis, MS: Concordia 1961), [W, 61–3] 367–8.

15 John Calvin, "Prefatory Address to King Francis" in *Institutes of the Christian Religion*, trans. and indexed by Ford L. Battles, vol. 20 of *The Library of Christian Classics*, ed. John T. McNeill (Philadelphia: The Westminster Press 1967), 16–7.

16 Benedict de Spinoza, *Theologico-Political Treatise*, in *The Chief Works of Benedict de Spinoza*, trans. R.H.M Elwes (London: George Bell & Sons 1883), 1: 93.

17 Ibid., 84.

18 Ibid., 85–7.

19 Thomas Hobbes, *Leviathan*, ed. and intro. by Richard Tuck (Cambridge: Cambridge University Press 1991), 306.

20 Blaise Pascal, *Pensées*, trans. and intro. by A.J. Krailsheimer (New York: Penguin 1966), no. 835, 286.

21 Colin Brown, *Miracles and the Critical Mind* (Grand Rapids, MI: Eerdmans 1984), 39–40.

22 I think that R.M. Burns is correct in seeing John Locke as being in the "moderate empiricist" tradition of these men. He is also correct to point out that "in spite of the broad tendencies of his [Locke's] thinking, which are clearly in line with moderate empiricism, his thought is characterized to some extent at least by the "egocentric predicament" which it shares with the Cartesians and Sceptics. One direct consequence of this is that his position on the question of the credibility of miracle stories is in significant respects far closer to that of Hume and the Deistic advocates of the *a priori* epistemological argument against miracles than that of either [Glanvill or Boyle]. *The Great Debate on Miracles* (London: Associated University Presses 1981), 59.

23 Ibid., 44.

24 Joseph Glanvill, *Sadducismus Triumphatus* (London 1689), 103.

25 Ibid., 124–5.

26 Cited by Burns, *Debate on Miracles*, 55, from Boyle Manuscripts, Royal Society, London, vol. 7, fol. 120–22.

27 Thomas Chubb, *Posthumous Works*, 2 vols. (London 1748), 2: 227.

28 David Hume, *Enquiries Concerning the Human Understanding and Concerning the Principles of Morals*,ed. L.A. Selby-Bigg, 2nd ed. (1902; Oxford 1972), 121–2. Hume's essay "Of Miracles" forms section 10 of the *Enquiry Concerning Human Understanding*.

29 Burns comments that "Part 2 of Hume's essay, with its four *a posteriori* arguments functions as a fairly compendious summary of all but

one of the major types of ... a posteriori arguments ... presented by the Deists." *Debate on Miracles*, 72.

30 See Joseph Butler, *The Analogy of Religion* (London 1736; reprint, New York: Frederick Ungar 1961), 142–49; Thomas Sherlock, *The Trial of the Witnesses of Jesus Christ* (London 1729), 58–64; William Wollaston, *Religion of Nature Delineated*, 2d ed. (London 1722), 56–8, Peter Annet, *Supernaturals Examined* (London 1747), 64–7.

31 See Burns, *Debate on Miracles*, 122–41.

32 Antony Flew goes so far as to claim that "The discussion starts from Hume. It was Hume, philosopher and future historian, who first raised the methodological question as to whether the occurrence of a genuinely miraculous event could possibly be known on historical evidence." See *God and Philosophy* (New York: Harcourt, Brace and World 1966), 145.

33 David Strauss, *Life of Jesus Critically Examined*, trans. George Eliot (1842; reprint, London: SCM Press 1973), ed. Peter C. Hodgson, no. 150, 777.

34 David Strauss, *A New Life of Jesus for the German People* (London: Williams and Norgate 1865), 1: xii.

35 Burns notes that "[v]ery many of the Deistic works were translated into German in the course of the eighteenth century (as well as many of the replies of the orthodox) and the ideas contained in them passed into German thought through Reimarus and others. *Debate on Miracles*, 276, n. 31.

36 John Henry Newman, *Two Essays on Biblical and Ecclesiastical Miracles* (London: Longmans, Green & Co. 1970), 17. The essay "The Miracles of Scripture" was written 1825–26 for the *Encyclopaedia Metropolitana*; the essay "The Miracles of Early Ecclesiastical History" was written in 1842–3. They were later combined into a single volume in 1870 and a new impression was reissued by Longmans, Green in 1911.

37 John Henry Newman, *Lectures on the Present Position of Catholics in England: Addressed to the Brothers of the Oratory in the Summer of 1851* (London: Burns, Oates and Co., n.d.), 306.

38 I am employing Colin Brown's translation of this passage from Ernst Troeltsch, *Gesammelte Schriften*, 2d ed., vol. 2 (1922; reprint, Darmstadt: Scientia Verlag Aalen 1962), 732. See Brown, *Miracles*, 129.

39 C.S. Lewis, *Surprised By Joy* (London: Geoffrey Bles 1955), 196.

40 Ibid., 196.

Questions of Miracle

1 The Logic of Probabilities in Hume's Argument against Miracles

FRED WILSON

The position is often stated that Hume's discussion of miracles is inconsistent with his views on the logical or ontological status of laws of nature and with his more general scepticism. Broad, for one, has so argued.[1] Hume's views on induction are assumed to go something like this. Any attempt to demonstrate knowledge of matters of fact presupposes causal reasoning, but causal reasoning is based not on any perception of necessary connections but on an unreasoned expectation that because events have been constantly conjoined in the past, they will be constantly conjoined in the future. The fact that our past experience gives rise to certain expectations provides absolutely no reason to think that these expectations will be fulfilled. But this view is forgotten as soon as Hume turns to the topic of miracles, where the argument requires certain assumptions about laws of nature. Here he claims that the laws of nature are based upon a firm and unalterable experience and dismisses what he apparently admits to be strong evidence for miracles on the basis of the claim that such events are absolutely impossible. The inconsistency between the discussion of miracles and the earlier discussions of induction and causality is said to be clear. Nonetheless, there is a certain implausibility to this claim that makes it difficult to entertain seriously, since it is unlikely that a philosopher as careful as Hume would have failed to recognize the inconsistency if it existed. What I propose to argue here is that there is in fact no inconsistency and that this becomes clear once one places the discussion of miracles in the broader context of the overall argument of the first *Enquiry*.[2] In particular, the charge of inconsistency disappears once one eliminates the caricature of Hume's views on causal reasoning upon which it rests.

To come to grips with the discussion of miracles in Hume it is necessary to place that discussion in its historical context.

In the generally empiricist atmosphere that developed in Britain following the mid-seventeenth-century civil wars, the general defence of the reasonableness of Christianity consisted of two parts.[3] First, it was held that rational argument, whether causal or teleological or both, could yield a reasonable belief that a deity of a more or less traditional sort existed. Then, second, in order to establish further that Jesus was the Son of God, it was held that one could rely upon a chain of testimony leading back from the present to the past to infer the existence of *miracles* testifying to the divinity of Jesus. Hume attacks this second inference in the essay on miracles and the first inference in the essay that follows in the *Enquiries* on God's particular providence (the themes of which are developed more fully in the *Dialogues concerning Natural Religion*). Given the central place that the appeal to miracles held in Christian apologetics in the seventeenth and eighteenth centuries, Hume's systematic attack on the argument from miracles constituted a clear attack on Christianity. To be sure, Hume's argument would never have persuaded John Wesley, but that would hardly have surprised Hume himself, nor should it surprise us: those in the grips of religious enthusiasm, whether it be John Wesley or Jimmy Swaggart, will hardly be persuaded by rational argument, however much it is still true that they *ought* to be persuaded by it.

The appeal to miracles to justify specifically Christian beliefs has a long history. One can find it already in the late Roman period in Eusebius.[4] Muslim thinkers were to challenge this traditional defence by arguing that chains of testimony become more unreliable the longer they become. As for their own Islamic beliefs, these, they admitted, had also to be justified by an appeal to miracles, but there was, it was claimed, a unique self-justifying miracle in the Koran, the specially revealed Word of God.[5] The critical theme of the Muslim apologists, that the longer a chain of testimony the less assurance it gives of the fact that a miracle has occurred, was developed in Britain in the seventeenth and eighteenth centuries.[6] It seems to have been introduced by the Oxford orientalist Edward Pocock, who had discovered this line of Muslim apologetics while studying in Alleppo.[7] It appears in Shaftesbury's *Characteristics* as part of the defence of deism,[8] to be criticized in Berkeley's *Alciphron*.[9] Craig gave it an unsound mathematical formulation,[10] to be followed by a reasonable analysis in terms of probability theory in an anonymous note, by George Hooper, in the *Philosophical Transactions of the Royal Society*.[11] This note received a popular and accurate description in Ephraim Chamber's *Cyclopaedia*,[12] a source undoubtedly known to Hume (as were Shaftesbury and Berkeley). Hume clearly knew this argument – he uses it in the *Treatise*[13] – but like Bayle (who knew Craig's essay) Hume does not rely upon it in his attack on miracles. This is not to say that Hume thought the argument unsound – in the *Treatise* he indicates clearly that he does think it to be, in general, a sound way of reasoning,[14] and furthermore it clearly lies behind his un-Scottish reservations on the authenticity of the Ossian poems.[15] In the case of miracles, however, it is not the increasing unreliability of a chain of testimony that Hume uses to attack religion, in spite of the fact that he finds the argument to be sound in general and in spite of the fact that he recognizes it to be a "very celebrated argument against the *Christian Religion*" (T 145). Instead, he raises the more general issue of whether *any* testimony, even of just *one* testifier, could ever render it reasonable to believe that a miracle had occurred. He argues, of course, that it cannot. The argument that he uses, however, is not separate from the sort of considerations drawn from probability theory that are used to establish that a chain of testimony provides less and less probable evidence the longer it becomes. Indeed, in his argument Hume appeals to another principle that also appears in the anonymous note in the *Philosophical Transactions*, one that deals with the probability that two independent pieces of testimony are both true, given the probabilities for each that they are true.

The relevant definition of "miracle" can be found in Locke's "Discourse on Miracles": "a sensible operation, which, being above the comprehension of the spectator, and in his opinion contrary to the established course of nature, is taken by him to be divine."[16] There are two points here that are prior to the inference that the event must be caused by the deity. The first is that the event must be beyond the comprehension of the spectator and the second is that the event is contrary to the established course of nature. Hume's discussion makes reference to both points. In particular, he adopts the Lockean criterion that a miracle is an event that violates the laws of nature (E 114). It follows that since, for Hume, to understand an event is to subsume it under a causal law, any miracle must be beyond the comprehension of the spectator. Hume's crucial move is to insist that simply because an event is somehow incomprehensible to a spectator, it does not follow that one can reasonably infer that it is a miracle, or even probably a miracle. Crucial to Hume's discussion of these points is his account of causation, or, what amounts to the same, his account of laws.

Here one must turn for detail to the *Treatise*. There are two definitions of "cause." The first defines cause objectively in terms of regularity.[17] On this definition there is no distinction between causal or lawful relations and accidental generalities.[18] This definition follows as a direct consequence of Hume's general argument against the rationalist ontology of objective necessary connections. Yet the notion of causation, Hume also insists, involves the idea of necessary connection.[19] This leads to the second definition of cause: a causal regularity, as opposed to one that is noncausal, that is, is an accidental generality, is one that we are prepared to use in making predictions and in supporting counterfactual inferences.[20] Thus, the moment of necessity that distinguishes causal from noncausal laws is subjective rather than objective. Not all causal judgments are rational, however: one must distinguish science from superstition. Those judgments are rational that conform to what Hume refers to as the "rules by which to judge of causes and effects" (T 173-6), that is, the rules of eliminative induction (Mill's Methods).[21]

As for why thought is rational when it conforms to these rules rather than those of superstition, or even the rule of induction by simple enumeration, Hume offers a pragmatic justification for those rules of experimental science arguing that they better serve our passion of curiosity, our cognitive interest in the truth.[22] It is misleading to suggest as many do[23] that Hume abandons the attempt to find a justification for scientific inferences and that he settles instead for a mere psychological explanation. To be sure, Hume does insist there is a psychological explanation for any and *all* our beliefs, both science and superstition, but science *alone* can satisfy our passion of curiosity or love of truth, and therefore science alone is *rationally justified*.[24] Of course, this defence of reason is not the a priori sort that the Cartesian insists upon – it is rather a posteriori and fallible – but Hume not only has no reason to accept the Cartesian standard, he in fact argues that it is an unreasonable cognitive standard![25]

Given Hume's general argument against objective necessary connections, there is no logical necessity attaching to any causal judgement; it is always possible that events will be contrary to any causal law. The human mind can therefore never achieve the level of absolute certainty that Cartesians and Aristotelians demand; all causal judgments are fallible. This amounts to scepticism provided one thinks that such standards as those of the Cartesian are reasonable. However, given the argument against objective necessities and, therefore, against the possibility of absolute certainty, it is not reasonable, Hume holds, to adopt the Cartesian standard. Hence, given the Humean argument, his position cannot reasonably be characterized as sceptical.

This means in particular that Hume's pragmatic justification or vindication of the norms of empirical science as the defining standards of human reason is itself empirical and fallible. This does not imply, however, that Hume is a sceptic about science or about causal inferences. For, if a sceptic is one who holds that no causal judgement is ever reasonable or that all are equally reasonable, then Hume is no sceptic.

Now, the *basic* evidence for a causal judgement that all *A*s are *B*s is the fact that all observed *A*s are *B*s. Often enough, however, we observe a certain contrariety in effects; that is, *A*s are sometimes followed by *B*s and sometimes by *C*s.[26] We do not in such cases, at least we do not if we are philosophers, simply conclude that there is no causality here, that here it is chance and not causation that is operative. Rather, we infer that *there is* a hitherto unknown factor, call it D^*, such that an *A* is *B* just in case it is D^* and is *C* just in case it is not D^*. We make this inference on the basis of our past successes in discovering previously unknown causal factors that can explain the contrariety of events.[27] The vulgar, of course, often *do* explain by appeal to chance the observed contrariety of effects: to use Hume's example, that my watch sometimes does not work properly is due to chance. But to the artisan such an explanation will not do: the artisan knows better. What stops the watch is not chance but a hidden – unknown but not unknowable – cause for example, a speck of dust.[28] Science, or what is the same for Hume, philosophy, has systematically extended the watchmaker's experience to many other cases and has been systematically successful in discovering causes for contrary effects. It is just this fact of experience, that science has been successful in discovering causes, that leads us to affirm the proposition, the law about laws to use Mill's phrase,[29] that for every event there is a cause, that is, the proposition that for every event there is a causal law under which it can be subsumed.[30]

Let us suppose, then, that we encounter an event that does not conform to the patterns that we have hitherto met in experience; for example, we may suppose that we are from the tropics and, going north, we encounter ice for the first time.[31] Here we run into a contrariety of effects in our experience. We thereby encounter an event that is, as Locke would say, beyond our comprehension, or, as Hume calls it in the essay on miracles, one that is marvellous. Yet we cannot count it a miracle. For we have the firm evidence of science that *there are* causes that account for this strange event.[32] It is, to be sure, not complete uniformity of experience that renders this judgement reasonable; after all, if there were complete uniformity there would be no contrariety. It is, rather, experience proceeding, as Hume says, "not *directly* ... but in an *oblique* manner" (T 133), that is, by inference from the law about laws, which says that for the contrary effects there are laws, even if we do not know them, that explain those effects.

And so, while Hume claims against the rationalist that it is always possible that there are events that do not have natural causes,[33] he also claims on the basis of unalterable experience that events that violate laws of nature are absolutely impossible.[34] Contrary to what Broad, for example, argues,[35] there is nothing inconsistent in this. Hume's discussion of laws in the essay on miracles hangs together with his more general discussion of laws and causation in the *Treatise*. Moreover, Hume can quite easily say that miracles can *conceivably* occur, while yet being impossible, again contrary to Broad's claim.[36] Finally, while it is true that for Hume laws are objectively nothing more than exceptionless regularities, it is also true that he allows laws, in particular laws about laws, to have logical forms more complicated than that of "All As are Bs." Laws about laws may include existential quantifications that enable one to infer the existence of an explanatory law even where one does not know specifically what it is.[37] And so the fact that we run across an event that violates a regular pattern of our experience provides evidence only that that pattern is not a law, but it does not falsify the belief that *there is* a law that explains it, for the latter can be inferred on the basis of our more general experience, which leads us to conclude that for any event there is a law that explains it.[38] Indeed, we all know from elementary logic classes that a single counterexample cannot falsify an existence claim! Thus, an event may be marvellous, and therefore, according to Locke's notion, beyond our comprehension, but at the same time not at all contrary, as Locke would also put it, to the established course of nature. Again contrary to Broad,[39] the fact that we discover exceptions to what we have previously thought to be regularities hardly testifies to there being events that are miracles, that is, events that violate laws of nature.

Since, as Hume holds, following Locke, a miracle is a violation of a law of nature, we can conclude that invariable and unalterable experience testifies to the impossibility of miracles. What, then, of the words of those who offer testimony that there are miracles?

In this case we have, on the one hand, the *testimony of reason* arguing that, since miracles are impossible, there are none. There is, on the other hand, the *testimony of some observer* that a miracle has occurred. *These two testimonies are in conflict.* Now, reason "must be consider'd as a kind of cause, of which truth is the natural effect," according to Hume (T 180),[40] in which case reason must be taken as providing one instance of testimony and the observer a second and independent instance. We have, then, two independent pieces of testimony.

The anonymous article in the *Philosophical Transactions of the Royal Society* dealt with this case in the second of its propositions.[41] (The first proposition dealt with chains of testimony.) The article reasons as follows. It lets each witness have a certain credibility, say p; p represents the relative frequency of saying the truth to saying "there remains but an assurance of $(1 - p)$ wanting to me, for the whole."[42] And "towards that the second attester contributes, according to his proportion of credibility"; that is, he contributes p of $(1 - p)$. Hence "there is now wanting but $(1 - p)$ of $(1 - p)$, that is $[(1 - p \times (1 - p)]$."[43] We therefore have

$$p^2: (1 - p)(1 - p)$$

as the ratio of truth-saying to false-saying. If we consider the case of testifiers with different credibilities (Proposition 3 of the anonymous article),[44] say p and p', then the ratio of truth-saying to false-saying is

$$(*)\quad pp': (1 - p)(1 - p').$$

The ratio of the truth-saying cases to the total number of cases

$$(+)\quad pp'/[pp' + (1 - p)(1 - p')]$$

will represent the probability of the two testifiers asserting the truth.[45] The formula (+) has been referred to as "Condorcet's formula,"[46] and the reasoning of the anonymous article that was used to justify the ratios has sufficient plausibility to be found repeated in its substance in Edgeworth's article on probability in the 11th edition of the *Encyclopaedia Britannica*.[47]

Now let the testimony of reason yield a probability p for the claim that a certain event occurred, and let p' be the testimony of an observer. It is evident from (*) that if the evidence of reason yields only a very small probability p that a miracle occurred, then the credibility p' of the observer must be very large indeed if it is to outweigh the testimony of reason.

As Hume mentions (E 108), the sort of consideration being made evident here was used by Archbishop Tillotson in his argument against transubstantiation.[48] Tillotson argued that the irresistible evidence of sense (irresistible, but not completely infallible!) testified against transubstantiation and that that evidence would systematically outweigh any claim that a miracle had occurred that testified to the truth of the papist doctrine.[49] Indeed, since the evidence for the occurrence of the miracle would, ultimately, have to be based upon evidence of sense, to accept on that basis the occurrence of the miracle testifying to transubstantiation and therefore to the unworthiness of sense experience would be to undercut the evidential basis for accepting that miracle. It would require a man to "renounce his senses at the same time that he relies upon them. For a man cannot believe a miracle without relying upon sense, nor transubstantiation, without renouncing it."[50] Hume generalizes this point that Christianity and transubstantiation are "ill-coupled," to argue that reason and miracles are similarly ill-coupled.

Reason, or at least empirical reason, is thought conforming to the "rules by which to judge causes"; that is, such habits of thought are those that are reasonable to have relative to the end established by our passion of curiosity or the love of truth. One of the rules that defines reason in this sense is the "same cause, same effect" rule that asserts that for every event there is a law that explains it.[51] Given that it is reasonable to accept the rules that define empirical reason, including this rule in particular, then one has accepted that miracles are, as one says, "contrary to reason." Reason in this sense is not infallible, but it cannot accept a miracle without subverting itself. Moreover, the evaluation of the credibility of witnesses is itself a matter of empirical reason – "The reason why we place any credit in witnesses and historians, is not derived from any *connexion*, which we perceive *a priori*, between testimony and reality, but because we are accustomed to find a conformity between them" (E 113). Reason uses observed relative frequencies of the contrary effects of truth-saying and false-saying together with probability theory to estimate the relative credibility of testifiers and combinations of testifiers. These inferences involve reasoning in terms of what Hume calls in the *Treatise* the "probability of causes" (T 130-42), and this reasoning presupposes ordinary causal reasoning in terms of the "rules by which to judge of causes" (T 132, 133).[52] The point is the simple one that these judgments are like ordinary causal inferences save that several relevant factors are not known explicitly. Their impact must therefore be estimated statistically rather than calculated directly.

It follows that the very capacity to estimate rationally the credibility of witnesses is undermined by the acceptance of any testimony that a miracle has occurred. Reason being a habit of thought, including the habit of thought that all events are law-governed, it follows that any belief in a miracle must be a miraculous belief that violates the habits of rational thought – it must, in other words, be itself a miracle. "I weigh the one miracle against the other; and according to the superiority, which I discover, I pronounce my decision, and always reject the greater miracle. If the falsehood of his testimony would be more miraculous, than the event which he relates; then, and not till then, can he pretend to command my belief or opinion" (E 116). But of course, the evaluation of witnesses is not merely a matter of the abstract calculation of probabilities. Truth-saying and false-saying are the contrary effects of several different causal factors, including, naturally, reason. To estimate the credibility of a witness, it is necessary to try to bring in and weigh these various factors – this, of course, is the point of cross-examining witnesses, and it is a point that any historian, Hume included, recognizes as he goes about evaluating the reliability of his sources. Mill, and Edgeworth following him, were to make this point;[53] and Condorcet was to discover its validity empirically, as he quite literally lost his head in the realization that it was not safe to assume that as the number of independent voters increased in the convention, the more likely it would be that the decision arrived at was the truth. It is this point that Hume goes on to develop in part 2 of the essay on miracles.

Hume here makes a variety of relevant points.[54] Miracles are reported in ages of credulity and superstition, not ages of science (E 119). External factors are relevant also, like the fact that rival religious traditions testify to different sorts of miracles that have contrary implications; in that context the contrary traditions cancel each other out, decreasing the credibility of both (E 121). There are, moreover, the various passions that lead us to depart from the rules of reason; we know these to be frequent enough to undermine the credibility of most testimony to miracles (E 117). In particular, given how miracles appeal to the very human passion of wonder, it should not at all surprise us that they have a continuing fascination for people. As Hume himself indicates, there *is* a natural tendency to accept miracles. It is, however, a tendency that aims at satisfying passions other than that of curiosity (E 117), and it is therefore not remarkable that people should have beliefs that are contrary to those that one would have if one conformed, like a good academic sceptic, to the rules that have as their end the discovery of truth and the satisfaction of our love of truth alone.

It is experience only, which gives authority to human testimony; and it is the same experience, which assures us of the laws of nature. When, therefore, these two kinds of experience are contrary, we have nothing to do but subtract the one from the other, and embrace an opinion, either on one side or the other, with that assurance which arises from the remainder. But according to the principle here explained, this subtraction, with regard to all popular religions, amounts to an entire annihilation; and therefore we may establish it as a maxim, that no human testimony can have such force as to prove a miracle, and make it a just foundation for any such system of religion. (E 127)

What is crucial through Hume's discussion of these points is that the estimation of the credibility of witnesses is itself a piece of causal reasoning.[55] In the end, the estimation of probabilities is parasitic upon the use of empirical reason as defined by the "rules by which to judge of causes" – as indeed Hume himself indicates when he discusses the probability of causes in the *Treatise*.

The general thrust of Hume's account of causal reasoning enables him to make a full reply to Price's critique of his essay,[56] even if one allows, as one no doubt should, that Hume did not fully appreciate the nature of Bayes' Theorem in probability theory.

Nothing in Hume's discussion turns upon his having known of Bayes' work – the source of his rules for combining probabilities of testimony derives far more probably from the anonymous article in the *Philosophical Transactions*. To apply Bayes' Theorem one must work in terms of conditional probabilities, whereas when Hume does discuss these things in the *Treatise*, it is clear that he is thinking in terms simply of the relative frequency of contrary effects.[57] Since he seems simply to apply these results straightforwardly to the case of testimony, with truth-saying and false-saying as contrary effects, it would appear that here, too, he is proceeding in terms of nonconditional rather than conditional probabilities, exactly as does the author of the anonymous note, but contrary to how he must be read if we are to make a Bayesian of him, as, for example, Owen and Sobel have tried to do, even in spite of their finding serious difficulties in that account[58] (for example, it cannot allow that the probability of a miracle is straight off *zero*[59]). From this it does not follow that Hume's account of how to combine probabilities of testimony, that is, the account of the anonymous note, is free from problems: it is not, as we have said following Mill and Edgeworth. But Hume saw this also, which is why he went on in part 2 of the essay to place these probability calculations in the broader context of an analysis of the factors that are causally relevant to the truth-saying and false-saying of witnesses. To suggest, as Price does, that in this context one can ignore the prior probabilities of events in estimating the worth of testimony[60] – so that the improbability of miracles cannot be used to count against the worthiness of testimony – is simply silly: the Roman proverb that Hume quotes from Plutarch, "I should not believe such a story were it told me by Cato" (E 113), makes the point forcefully enough. Price, moreover, simply misunderstands parts of Hume's discussion. Thus, for example, he suggests that the antecedent probability of miracles is no greater than that of electricity or magnetism before they were discovered.[61] But this is to miss the point that, while these phenomena may constitute marvels, they do not constitute miracles; nor did the relevant phenomena suggest anything of the miraculous before science succeeded in explaining them. Rather, what science was committed to, prior to successfully advancing explanations, was that these phenomena had not yet been explained but that we had good reason, based on past experience, to believe that *there were* laws that explained them. It is precisely this last commitment that is by definition absent in the case of miracles.

What Price's discussion evidences is the presence of the notion of a natural law for which there could be exceptions.[62] It is precisely this notion that Hume is concerned to argue against. Within the context of an Aristotelian or a Cartesian metaphysics, this notion in fact makes sense. But Hume argued systematically against these positions and defended the alternative view that, objectively, all that causation amounts to is matter-of-fact *regularity*. Once he has done this and once he has vindicated the practice of science as including the rule that for any event *there is* a law that explains it, then there is simply no place for a miracle to occur, nor any plausibility to testimony that one has witnessed one: "a miracle, supported by any human testimony, [is] more properly a subject of derision than of argument" (E 124). *Science and miracles – science and Christianity – are inconsistent: one cannot be both rational and Christian.* It is *this* thesis that Hume aimed to establish, and he more or less succeeded.

NOTES

1 C.D. Broad, "Hume's Theory of the Credibility of Miracles," *Proceedings of the Aristotelian Society* n.s. 17 (1916–17): 77–94.
2 David Hume, *Enquiries Concerning the Human Understanding and Concerning the Principles of Morals*, ed. L.A. Selby-Bigge, 2d ed. (1902; Oxford, 1972). Further references ("E") will be given in parentheses within the body of the text.
3 Cf. R.M. Burns, *The Great Debate on Miracles* (Lewisburg, PA, 1981).
4 Eusebius Pamphili, Bishop of Caesarea, *The Proof of the Gospel (Demonstatio Evengelica)*, trans. W.J. Ferrar, 2 vols. (London, 1920); see especially bk. 3.
5 One can find exemplifications of this controversy repeated up into the nineteenth century; see S. Lee, *Controversial Tracts on Christianity and Mohammedanism by the Late Rev. Henry Martyn* (Cambridge, 1824). In his volume Lee translates an arabic tract by Mirza Ibrahim. It was to this that Henry Martyn wrote several replies; these are the "controversial tracts" that Lee is collecting and editing. But in addition, Lee includes a translation of a rejoinder to Martyn by Mohammed Ruza of Hamadan, together with a lengthy discussion of the same issues by Lee himself.

What we are interested in here is the case that Islamic scholars made for their religion, the case, that is, in the tract by Mirza Ibrahim. According to this tract, assurance is of the first importance since for the defenders of any faith, "in the matter of a prophetic mission, nothing less than assurance can be admitted as of any weight" (11); "the reality of a prophetic mission cannot be established, in the estimation of those who are not Prophets, but by the production of a miracle" (2). The required miracle is the Koran itself. Now the Arabs knew the science of eloquence; "had therefore [Mohammed's] production originated in this science, they [the Arabs] could have produced its equal" (10). But they have not; "in fact, no one of them, during the space of twelve hundred years, has yet produced the like, notwithstanding the continued allegations of the preachers of Islamism, that the Koran holds out a challenge to all" (10–11). The required assurance, then, "is to be obtained from an acquaintance with the sciences of eloquence, which must be founded upon a knowledge of the elements of language, just as it is from the unanimous consent of the learned; namely, that it is a miracle, and not the effect of eloquence alone: – an assurance, in which there can remain no doubt; and not less convincing than that of the miracles of the other Prophets. Nay, it is more so; for the impossibility of imitation is now just what it was at the first performance of the miracle, on account of its perpetuity, and its utter incapability of decay. And further, it will for ever remain just what it was at the first propagation if Islamism, contrary to the character of the miracles of other Prophets, of which we have now nothing remaining but mere relations, as Moses or Jesus, for instance, did this or that; or it is thus preserved by tradition. But no relation can have the evidence of an eyewitness. The miracles of the other Prophets, moreover, in addition to their want of evidence, as already noticed, when compared with that of the Koran, will by length of time become less and less convincing; because in process of time any relation must become less impressive. But the miracle of the Koran, on the contrary, will, in process of time, become more so, because the learned who have confessed their inability to produce the like, will have been more numerous, though the miracle itself will remain exactly what it was at the first: and the conviction of its being a miracle will thus become more powerful. Hence will the mystery be explained, why this Prophet was, to the exclusion of others, termed the seal of prophecy: because, as the evidence of their miracles is daily becoming weaker, a time must at last arrive, when it will fail of affording assurance, that they were miracles at all; whence would arise the necessity of the mission of another prophet and other miracles, 'lest men should have an argument of excuse against God after the Apostles had been sent to them' [Sale's Koran, 1:117]: contrary to what is the fact, as it respects this Prophet and his miracles; which will remain to the day of judgment, not only what it was at the first, but more convincing. And hence there will be no necessity for another Prophet, or for other miracles to all eternity" (12–14).

6 Not surprisingly, the British thinkers did not develop the positive theme that the Koran was a self-validating miracle that justified the

claims of Islam against those of the Christians.

7 See Edward Pocock, *Specimen Historiae Arabum* (Oxford, 1650), 195; this is the Arabic text and Latin translation of a work by Frighor (Abu al-Faraj) called *Bar Hebraeus*.

8 Anthony, Earl of Shaftesbury, *Characteristics of Men, Manners, Opinions, Times*, ed. J. M. Robertson, 2 vols. (1711; Indianapolis, 1964). Shaftesbury writes: "It belongs to mere enthusiasts and fanatics to plead the sufficiency of a reiterate translated text, derived through so many channels and subjected to so many variations, of which they are wholly ignorant" (2:302).

   Shaftesbury indicates familiarity with the Islamic position that Pocock had introduced: "The Mahometan clergy seem to have a different policy. They boldly rest the foundation of their religion on a book: such a one (according to their pretension) is not only perfect, but inimitable." Shaftesbury makes short work of this idea: he continues, "Were a real man of letters and a just critic permitted to examine this scripture by the known rules of art, he would soon perhaps refute this plea" (301).

9 George Berkeley, *Alciphron*, in *The Works of George Berkeley*, ed. A.A. Luce and T.E. Jessop, vol. 3 (London, 1732; Edinburgh, 1950). The argument is expressed in the dialogue by the main character, Alciphron: "Do you not see ... that all this hangs by tradition? And tradition, take my word for it, gives but a weak hold: it is a chain whereof the first links may be stronger than steel, and yet the last as weak as wax, and brittle as glass. Imagine a picture copied successively by a hundred painters, one from another, how like must the last copy be to the original! How lively and distinct will an image be, after a hundred reflexions between two parallel mirrors! Thus like and thus lively do I think a faint vanishing tradition, at the end of sixteen or seventeen hundred years. Some men have a false heart, others a wrong head; and, where both are true, the memory may be treacherous. Hence there is still something added, something omitted, and something varied from the truth: and the sum of many such additions, deductions and alterations accumulated for several ages doth, at the foot of the account, make quite another thing" (222). Berkeley goes on to argue (222ff.) for the unsoundness of this case for the unreliability of the argument for Christian beliefs based on tradition, that is, on chains of testimony.

   In this discussion of "free thinkers" in *Alciphron*, Berkeley clearly has Shaftesbury in mind. Shaftesbury is one possible source of his knowledge of the sceptical argument from the regress of testimony. There is another possible source: Pocock was a friend of and corresponded with Archbishop Marsh of Dublin, whom Berkeley must undoubtedly have known when he was a student at Trinity College.

10 John Craig, "Theologiae Christianae Principia Mathematica," in *Craig's Rule of Historical Evidence, History and Theory*, trans. G. Nadel, Beiheft 4 (1699; The Hague, 1964). See F. Wilson, "The Origins of Hume's Sceptical Argument against Reason," *History of Philosophy Quarterly* 2 (1985): 323–35.

11 "A Calculation of the Credibility of Human Testimony," *Philosophical Transactions of the Royal Society of London* 21 (1699). The attribution to Hooper was first (re)discovered apparently by Brown Grier, in an unpublished manuscript of 1982 on "George Hooper and the Early Theory of Testimony"; see the reference in Stephen Stigler, "John Craig and the Probability of History: From the Death of Christ to the Birth of Laplace," *Journal of the American Statistical Association* 81 (1986), 879–87. See also George Hooper, "A Fair and Methodical Discussion of the First and Great Controversy between the Church of England and the Church of Rome concerning the Infallible Guide," in *The Works of the Right Reverend George Hooper D.D.*, vol. 1 (1757; reprint Oxford, 1855).

12 Ephraim Chambers, "Certitude," in *Cyclopaedia* (London, 1746). When the thesis of this article is joined to the thesis of the article on "Tradition," one has the attack on Christianity that one finds in the Muslim thinkers, in Shaftesbury, and in Berkeley.

13 It is the basis of Hume's well-known sceptical argument against reason in *A Treatise of Human Nature*, ed. L.A. Selby-Bigge, 2nd ed. (1888; Oxford, 1987), 180ff. (Further references ["T"] will be given in parentheses within the body of the text.) I have discussed this particular argument in detail in "Hume's Sceptical Argument against Reason," *Hume Studies* 9 (November 1983): 90–129, and in "Is Hume a Sceptic with regard to Reason?" *Philosophy Research Archives* 10 (1984): 275–320. Hume mentions the argument based on a long chain of testimonies earlier in the Treatise (145–6), and in a footnote (T 146) he indicates that the sceptical argument against reason has the form of this regress of testimony. I have argued in "Hume's Sceptical Argument" that we should take Halley's treatment as the most reasonable source for Hume's discussion.

14 "Every new probability diminishes the original conviction; and however great that conviction may be suppos'd, 'tis impossible it

can subsist under such re-iterated diminutions. This is true in general" (T 145).

15 In the unpublished essay "Of the Authenticity of Ossian's Poems," in David Hume, *The Philosophical Works*, ed. T.H. Green and T.H. Grose, 4 vols. (Oxford, 1882), 4:415–24, Hume writes, "they were composed, you say, in the Highlands, about fifteen centuries ago; and have been faithfully transmitted, ever since, by oral tradition, through ages totally ignorant of letters, by the rudest, perhaps of all the European nations; the most necessitous, the most turbulent, the most ferocious, and the most unsettled. Did ever any event happen that approached within a hundred degrees of this mighty wonder, even to the nations them most fortunate in their climate and situation? Can a ballad be shown that has passed, uncorrupted, by oral tradition, through three generations among the Greeks, or Italians, or Phoenicians, or Eyptians, or even among the natives of such countries as Otaheite or Molacca, who seem exempted by nature from all attention but to amusement, to poetry, and music?" (416).

Hume was to continue his respect for the argument as applied to the Ossian poems until the end of his life: in 1776 he wrote to Gibbon that "I see you entertain a great Doubt with regard to the Authenticity of the Poems of Ossian. You are certainly right in so doing. It is, indeed, strange, that any men of Sense could have imagin'd it possible, that above twenty thousand Verses, along with numberless historical Facts, could have been preserv'd by oral Tradition during fifty Generations, by the rudest, perhaps of all European Nations; the most necessitous, the most turbulent, and the most unsettled. Where a Supposition is so contrary to common Sense, any positive Evidence of it ought never to be regarded. Men run with great Avidity to file their Evidence in favour of what flatters their Passions, and their national Prejudices. You are, therefore, over and above indulgent to us in speaking of the Matter with Hesitation" (David Hume, *The Letters of David Hume*, ed. J.Y.T. Grieg [Oxford, 1932], 3:310–11).

16 J. Locke, *The Reasonableness of Christianity*, ed. I.T. Ramsey (Stanford, CA, 1958), 33. Similar definitions were offered by others of the age. Thus, Samuel Clarke, in his Boyle Lectures, defined a miracle as "a work effected in a manner ... different from the common and regular method of providence, by the interposition either of God himself, or of some intelligent agent superior to men" (*The Works of Samuel Clarke* [London, 1738], 2:701). Bishop Butler remarks that "a

miracle, in its very notion, is relative to a course of nature; and implies somewhat different from it, considered as being so" (*The Works of Joseph Butler*, ed. W.E. Gladstone [Oxford, 1896], 1:214).

Hume himself states that "A miracle may be accurately defined, *a transgression of a law of nature by a particular volition of the Deity, or by the interposition of some invisible agent*" (E 115, n. 1).

17 A cause, upon this definition, is "*an object precedent and contiguous to another, and where all the objects resembling the former are plac'd in a like relation of priority and contiguity to those objects, that resemble the latter*" (T 172); or, it is "*an object, followed by another, and where all the objects similar to the first are followed by objects similar to the second*" (E 76).

18 Cf. F. Wilson, *Laws and Other Worlds* (Dordrecht, 1986).

19 "An object may be contiguous and prior to another, without being consider'd as its cause. There is a NECESSARY CONNEXION to be taken into consideration; and that relation is of much greater importance, than any of the other two above-mention'd" (T 77).

20 Upon this definition a cause is "an object precedent and contiguous to another, and so united with it in the imagination, that the idea of the one determines the mind to form the idea of the other, and the impression of the one to form a more lively idea of the other" (T 172); or "an object followed by another, and whose appearance always conveys the thought to that other" (E 77).

21 Hume's is the best statement of 'Mill's Methods' between Bacon and Herschel. See also F. Wilson, "Is There a Prussian Hume?" *Hume Studies* 8 (April 1982): 1–18; and F. Wilson, "'Rules by Which to Judge of Causes' before Hume," *Monist* (forthcoming).

22 For the details of this pragmatic "vindication," see F. Wilson, "Hume's Defence of Causal Inference," *Dialogue* 22 (1983): 661–94.

23 For example, Broad, "Hume's Theory," 91–2.

24 Cf. F. Wilson, "Hume's Defence of Science," *Dialogue* 25 (1986): 611–28.

25 Cf. F. Wilson, "Hume's Cognitive Stoicism," *Hume Studies* 10, supplement (1985): 521–48.

26 "But as 'tis frequently found, that one observation is contrary to another, and that causes and effects follow not in the same order, of which we have had experience, we are oblig'd to vary our reasoning on account of this uncertainty, and take into consideration the contrariety of events" (T 131).

"One, who in our climate, should expect better weather in any week of June than in one of December, would reason justly, and conformably to experience; but it is certain, that he may happen, in the event, to find himself mistaken. However, we may observe, that, in such a case, he would have no cause to complain of experience; because it commonly informs us beforehand of the uncertainty, but that contrariety of events, which we may learn from a diligent observation. All effects follow not with like certainty from their supposed causes. Some events are found, in all countries and all ages, to have been constantly conjoined together: Others are found to have been more variable, and sometimes to disappoint our expectations; so that, in our reasonings concerning matter of fact, there are all imaginable degrees of assurance, from the highest certainty to the lowest species of moral evidence" (E110).

27 "From the observation of several parallel instances, philosophers form a maxim, that the connexion betwixt all causes and effects is equally necessary, and that its seeming uncertainty in some instances proceeds from the secret opposition of contrary causes" (T 132).

28 "A peasant can give no better reason for the stopping of any clock or watch than to say, that commonly it does not go right: But an artisan easily perceives, that the same force in the spring or pendulum has always the same influence on the wheels; but fails of its usual effect, perhaps by reason of a grain of dust, which puts a stop to the whole movement" (T132).

29 John Stuart Mill, *System of Logic*, 8th ed. (London, 1872), 3.5.2, 3.21.2, 3.

30 On the logic of this inference, see F. Wilson, *Causation, Explanation and Deduction* (Dordrecht, 1985), 1.2, 1.3; "Kuhn and Goodman: Revolutionary vs. Conservative Science," *Philosophical Studies* 44 (1983): 369–80.

31 This is, of course, the example that Hume himself uses in the essay on miracles: "The Indian prince, who refused to believe the first relations concerning the effects of frost, reasoned justly; and it naturally required very strong testimony to engage his assent to facts, that arose from a state of nature, with which he was unacquainted, and which bore so little analogy to those events, of which he had had constant and uniform experience, they were not conformable to it" (E 113–14).

32 "[W]hen any cause fails of producing its usual effect, philosophers ascribe not this to any irregularity in nature; but suppose, that some secret causes, in the particular structure of parts, have prevented the operation" (E 58).

33 Thus, that the proposition that "Whatever has a beginning has also
    a cause of *existence* ... is utterly incapable of a demonstrative proof,
    we may satisfy ourselves by considering, that as all distinct ideas
    are separable from each other, and as the ideas of cause and effect
    are evidently distinct, 'twill be easy for us to conceive any object to
    be non-existent this moment, and existent the next, without con-
    joining to it the distinct idea of a cause or productive principle. The
    separation, therefore, of the idea of a cause from that of a begin-
    ning of existence, is plainly possible for the imagination; and conse-
    quently the actual separation of these objects is so far possible, but
    it implies no contradiction nor absurdity; and is therefore incapable
    of being refuted by any reasoning from mere ideas; without which
    'tis impossible to demonstrate the necessity of a cause" (T 79–80).
    "The mind can never possibly find the effect in the supposed
    cause, by the most accurate scrutiny and examination. For the ef-
    fect is totally different from the cause, and consequently can never
    be discovered in it" (E 29).

34 "It is universally allowed that matter, in all its operations, is actu-
    ated by a necessary force, and that every natural effect is so pre-
    cisely determined by the energy of its cause that no other effect, in
    such particular circumstances, could possibly have resulted from it.
    The degree and direction of every motion is, by the laws of nature,
    prescribed with such exactness that a living creature may as soon
    arise from the shock of two bodies as motion in any other degree
    of direction than what is actually produced by it" (E 82).

35 Broad, "Hume's Theory," 91.

36 Ibid., 93–4.

37 Cf. Wilson, *Causation, Explanation and Deduction* and "Kuhn and
    Goodman."

38 Broad, "Hume's Theory," 90, does recognize this point but does not
    see its importance.

39 Broad, 93–4.

40 "[O]ur assurance in any argument of this kind [an argument de-
    rived from human testimony and the reports of eye-witnesses and
    spectators] is derived from no other principle than our observation
    of the veracity of human testimony, and of the usual conformity of
    facts to the reports of witnesses. It being a general maxim, that no
    objects have any discoverable connexion together, and that all the
    inferences, which we can draw from one to another, are founded
    merely on our experience of their constant and regular conjunction;

it is evident, that we ought not to make an exception to the maxim in favour of human testimony, whose connexion with any event seems, in itself, as little necessary as any other" (E 111).

41 "Credibility of Human Testimony," 361-2.

42 The article puts it in terms of what one would be willing to wager: "*Moral Certitude Incompleat*, has its several Degrees to be estimated by the Proportion it bears to the *Absolute*. As if one in whom I have that degree of Confidence, as that I would not give above One in Six to be ensur'd of the Truth of what he says, shall inform me ... concerning 1200£: I may then reckon that I have as good as the Absolute Certainty of a 1000£, or five sixths of Absolute Certainty for the whole Summ" (Ibid., 359).

43 Ibid., 361.

44 Ibid., 362.

45 This formula can also be given an interpretation in which p and p' are taken to be conditional probabilities, rather than absolute or nonconditional probabilities as the author of the anonymous note in the Royal Society *Transactions*. The formula understood in terms of conditional probabilities can be easily derived from Bayes' Theorem: cf. D. Owen, "Hume versus Price on Miracles and Prior Probabilities: Testimony and the Bayesian Calculation," *Philosophical Quarterly* 37 (1987): 191n. Owen proposes that Hume be construed as using conditional probabilities and that he used the formula (+) so understood in the argument against miracles. But wherever Hume speaks of probabilities, it is clear that he is thinking, as is the author of the anonymous note, in nonconditional terms (for example, T 124ff.). That means that in attempting to interpret Hume we must, contrary to Owen, understand (+) and (*) in nonconditional terms.

46 Cf. Ilkka Niiniluoto, "L.J. Cohen versus Bayesianism," *The Behavioral and Brain Sciences* 4 (1981): 349-50. For Condorcet, see Marie-Jean-Antoine-Nicolas Caritat, Marquis de Condorcet, "Mémoire sur le calcul des probabilités," section five of which is entitled, "Sur les probabilitiés des faits extraordinaires," in *Histoire de l'académie royale des sciences* (1786), 554-5. As Isaac Todhunter (*A History of the Mathematical Theory of Probability* [Cambridge, 1895; New York, 1965]) observes (400), Condorcet gives his formula "with every little explanation"; it is therefore not exactly clear how he has arrived at it. The anonymous note in the Royal Society *Transactions* is more clear on this point.

47 Francis Y. Edgeworth, *Encyclopaedia Britannica*, 11th ed., s.v. "probability."

48 John Tillotson, "Sermon 26," in *Works* (London, 1820), 2:407–52.

49 Ibid., 447ff.

50 Ibid., 449.

51 See Wilson, "A Prussian in Hume?"

52 For a detailed analysis of these inferences, see Wilson, "Hume's Sceptical Argument."

53 Mill, *System of Logic*, 3.18.3; Edgeworth, "Probability."

54 These he has already summarized in part 1 of the essay: "This contrariety of evidence, in the present case, may be derived from several different causes; from the opposition of contrary testimony; from the character or number of the witnesses; from the manner of their delivering their testimony; or from the union of all these circumstances. We entertain a suspicion concerning any matter of fact, when the witnesses contradict each other; when they are but few, or of a doubtful character; when they have an interest in what they affirm; when they deliver their testimony with hesitation, or on the contrary, with too violent asseverations. There are many other particulars of the same kind, which may diminish or destroy the force of any argument, derived from human testimony" (E 112–13).

55 "Were not the memory tenacious to a certain degree, had not men commonly an inclination to truth and a principle of probity; were they not sensible to shame, when detected in a falsehood: Were not these, I say, discovered by *experience* to be qualities, inherent in human nature, we should never repose the least confidence in human testimony. A man delirious, or noted for falsehood and villany, has no manner of authority with us" (E 112).

56 Richard Price, "On the Importance of Christianity, the Nature of Historical Evidence, and Miracles," in *Four Dissertations*, 5th ed. (Harlow, 1811).

57 He adopts the classical or ignorance view of probability that was later to be defended in detail by Laplace; cf. T 125–6.

58 Owen, "Hume versus Price"; J.H. Sobel, "On the Evidence of Testimony for Miracles: A Bayesian Interpretation of David Hume's Analysis," *Philosophical Quarterly* 37 (1987): 166–86.

59 And this is clearly what Hume means to assert about miracles when he states that "as a uniform experience amounts to a proof, there is here a direct and full *proof*, from the nature of the fact, against the existence of any miracle" (E 115).

60 Price, "Importance of Christianity," 234ff. For comments on Price's case from the context of the Bayesian perspective of Price himself, see Sobel, "Testimony for Miracles," 177ff.

61 Ibid., 244.

62 Price waffles here. He considers the usual "supposition that a miracle ... implies a *violation* or *suspension* of the laws of nature" and argues, "But, in reality, this is by no means necessarily included in the idea of a miracle. A sensible and *extraordinary effect* produced by *superior power*, no more implies that a law of nature is violated, than any *common effect* produced by *human power*" (253). However, while this allows that there can be miracles that do not involve violations of any law of nature, it does so only at the cost of extending the notion of "law of nature" to include *non-sensible* factors among those that are covered by the laws. But this already is excluded by Locke and by Hume, who both insist that if the relevant force is non-sensible then the event is a miracle. Thus, as Hume puts it, "A miracle may by accurately defined, *a transgression of a law of nature by a particular volition of the Deity, or by the interposition of some invisible agent*" (E 115, n. 1).

Price's suggestion that God can be treated as a non-natural cause that intervenes in the course of events without violating laws of nature in the way in which humans intervene in the course of events without violating laws has recently been revived by Robert Larmer in "Miracles and the Laws of Nature," this volume, chap. 3. The problem does not concern the nature of agency, as Larmer suggests, but rather the intelligibility of the idea of a supra-sensible or non-natural cause. But in any case, the suggestion does not establish that there can be miracles that do not violate laws of nature, since God's intervention will still violate the *order of natural causes*, the regularities governing sensible occurrences, and as Locke and Hume indicate, it is precisely this that the Christian needs and uses to justify his claims.

2 David Hume and the Miraculous

ROBERT LARMER

In his discussion of the logic of probabilities in Hume's argument against miracles (this volume, chap. 1), Fred Wilson attempts to refute the view that Hume's discussion of miracles is inconsistent with his earlier discussions of induction and causality. Wilson finds it difficult to entertain this claim seriously, "since it is unlikely that a philosopher as careful as Hume would have failed to recognize the inconsistency if it existed," and he argues that it rests upon a caricature of Hume's views on causal reasoning. He feels that once Hume's discussion of miracles is placed in the context of the overall argument of the first *Enquiry*, it becomes impossible to raise the charge of inconsistency.

Little weight can be placed on his suggestion that a philosopher as careful as Hume is unlikely to be guilty of inconsistency. It is unwise to be overhasty in attributing inconsistency to a philosopher of Hume's calibre, but it is scarcely unknown that the greatest thinkers are occasionally guilty in this regard, and there seems no reason to assume that Hume is incapable of such slips. The real question is whether the text supports the interpretation Wilson wishes to advance. The answer is that it does not.

One of the first points where this becomes obvious is with his claim that Hume's crucial move in the essay "Of Miracles" "is to insist that simply because an event is somehow incomprehensible to a spectator, it does not follow that one can rea-

sonably infer that it is a miracle, or even probably a miracle."
This is a popular view to attribute to Hume, but it is a product
of eisegesis not exegesis, and it is significant that in an article
crammed with references, Wilson simply asserts it, making no
reference to the text.

Even the most superficial reading of the essay makes clear that
Hume was convinced that if certain events were to occur, they
could be correctly identified as miracles. It is precisely this conviction that underlies the distinction he attempts to draw between what is merely marvellous and what is miraculous.[1] He
is quite prepared to say that "it is a miracle that a dead man
should come to life"(E 115; see also his comments on the death
of Queen Elizabeth, E 128). In the present context, the issue
is not whether Hume is entitled to make this distinction between
the merely marvellous and the genuinely miraculous but what
is the aim of his argument. His purpose is not to establish that
if a dead person came back to life, we could not be sure that
the event was a miracle, but rather that rational belief in such
an event could never be justified on the basis of testimonial
evidence.

Wilson goes wrong in confusing two logically distinct questions: How much testimonial evidence is needed to establish the
occurrence of an unusual event? and On what basis could it
be established that an unusual event is a miracle? Wilson takes
Hume to be addressing the second question and interprets him
as arguing that it is impossible to justify belief that an unusual
event is a violation of the laws of nature. On Wilson's reading,
Hume's argument is directed not at the difficulties of establishing
unusual events on the basis of testimonial evidence but at the
impossibility of ever rationally believing that an unusual event
constitutes a violation of the laws of nature.

Unfortunately, this reading makes nonsense not only of
Hume's explicit willingness to identify certain conceivable events
as miracles but also of his emphasis on the inability of testimonial
evidence to establish such events. If Wilson's reading is accepted,
it becomes a mystery why Hume would even concern himself
with issues of testimony, since the argument would establish that
no matter what the unusual event, it is always irrational to view
it as a violation of the laws of nature. It is certainly possible
to formulate an argument against miracles along the line Wilson

takes, but it is not Hume's argument, and we do ourselves a disservice if we conflate the two.[2]

This misinterpretation of Hume infects Wilson's treatment of Hume's critics.[3] He takes C.D. Broad to task for failing to recognize that "the fact that we discover exceptions to what we have previously thought to be regularities hardly testifies to these being events that are miracles, that is, events that violate laws of nature." This is to ignore the fact that Broad explicitly makes this point and can scarcely be accused of failing to recognize its importance.[4]

What Broad recognizes and Wilson fails to recognize and what must be taken into account in any discussion of whether Hume's treatment of miracles is consistent with his more general scepticism is that his argument is directed not at demonstrating that it is irrational to believe that unusual events violate the laws of nature but at showing we could never have sufficient testimonial evidence to justify belief in miracles. Put a little differently, Hume's aim is to argue not that if the Resurrection occurred, it would be irrational to view it as a violation of the laws of nature but that testimonial evidence could never justify belief in the Resurrection.

His argument in support of this conclusion is that miracles are unusual events and that there are insurmountable difficulties to establishing such unusual events on the basis of testimonial evidence. A problem he faces, however, is that the class of unusual events is not exhausted by miracles and that we quite often accept the occurrence of unusual events on the basis of testimonial evidence. On pain of his argument proving too much, he must argue not that it is in general impossible to establish the occurrence of unusual events on the basis of testimonial evidence but that it is impossible to establish the occurrence of a special type of unusual event, that is, miracles, on the basis of such evidence. He tries to do this by drawing a distinction between marvels and miracles on the ground that an event that is a marvel is unusual, but it does not contradict our firm and unalterable experience, that is, the laws of nature, whereas a miracle does contradict that experience, that is, it violates the laws of nature (E 114).[5]

In the context of our present discussion, two points are important. The first is that this distinction will not do the job Hume wants it to. Hume wants to be able to accept marvels on the ground that, although they are contrary to our ordinary experience, deeper investigation will establish they do not really contradict the laws of nature. Miracles, on the other hand, contradict our unalterable experience and thus constitute violations of the laws of nature.

The problem, if one wants to say with Hume that marvels can be established on the basis of testimonial evidence but that miracles cannot, is that unless one becomes convinced of the occurrence of an unusual event, one is scarcely likely to conduct the deeper investigation that will establish that it does not violate the laws of nature. In other words, unless testimonial evidence can persuade one that the unusual event occurred, there will be no reason, in the absence of personally witnessing the event, to search for its explanation. Marvels, therefore, are in no more privileged an epistemological position than miracles.

The second point is that it is difficult to see how Hume can use the term "unalterable experience" and remain consistent with his earlier treatment of induction and causality. As is well known, he argued that beliefs about matters of fact can never be demonstrated, since "[t]he contrary of every matter of fact is still possible; because it can never imply a contradiction, and is conceived by the mind with the same facility and distinctness, as if ever so conformable to reality" (E 25). Any attempt to demonstrate knowledge concerning matters of fact must presuppose causal reasoning, but causal reasoning is based not on any genuine perception of necessary connections but on an unreasoned expectation that because events have been constantly conjoined in the past, they will be constantly conjoined in the future. Thus, "[i]t is impossible ... that any arguments from experience can prove ... resemblance of the past to the future; since all these arguments are founded on the supposition of that resemblance ... In vain do you pretend to have learned the nature of bodies from your past experience" (E 38). The fact that our past experience gives rise to certain expectations provides absolutely no reason to think that these expectations will be fulfilled.

On the basis of the passages we have just examined, one would expect that for Hume, a law of nature amounts simply to the claim that in the past there has existed a constant conjunction between certain perceptions. It is scarcely surprising that certain expectations will accompany such claims, but these are simply a consequence of our psychology and not based upon any insight into the nature of reality.

These earlier remarks concerning causality and induction seem to be forgotten, however, when Hume begins to consider the subject of miracles and is led to make explicit claims concerning the laws of nature. Here we find him claiming that the laws of nature are based on a firm and unalterable experience. How our experience can be unalterable is never explained, but Hume's conception of a law of nature seems to be that it is a regularity of nature that we know can never have exceptions.

The problem, of course, is that it is not easy to see how Hume, of all people, has any right to appeal to the idea of unalterable experience. Two suggestions are often put forward by those sympathetic to his views, but neither seems adequate.

The first is that neither the scepticism inherent in his treatment of causality and induction nor the dogmatism characteristic of his explicit statements in the tenth chapter of the *Enquiry* represents his true view concerning the laws of nature. Rather, in order to arrive at his true view, we must examine his account of probable reasoning and its grounding in human psychology. When we do this, it is suggested, we find that he never denied that the idea of necessary connection is an essential element of probable reasoning but simply insisted that this idea is grounded in human psychology, not in nature itself. It is a mistake, therefore, to think that he does not have the resources to distinguish between genuine laws of nature and simple numerically universal propositions.

There are several reasons why this is not a promising approach. First, Hume's most explicit remarks concerning the laws of nature occur in his discussion of the rationality of belief in miracles in chapter 10. It is exegetically suspect to ignore his explicit treatment of the laws of nature in this essay on miracles in hopes of deriving a more palatable alternative from a different portion of his philosophy. Moreover, it must be emphasized that deriving a more palatable alternative would not absolve him of the charge of inconsistency, since it would remain true that it is not the concept of natural law he is working with in chapter 10. The issue is not whether Hume could have developed a concept of the laws of nature consistent with his treatment of induction and causality or whether such a concept can be found elsewhere in his work but whether the concept actually employed in the essay on miracles is consistent with his treatment of induction and causality.

Second, even if one could extract a different concept of the laws of nature and substitute it for the one Hume employs in the essay, it would not resolve his problems. It is essential, if his argument is not to be guilty of proving too much, for him to be able to distinguish between marvels considered as unusual events and miracles considered as unusual events. He does this on the grounds that further investigation will reveal that marvels, unlike miracles, do not really violate the laws of nature.

What Hume and critics such as Wilson seem to have missed is that the question of whether an event occurred is logically distinct from the question of whether further investigation will show that it does not violate the laws of nature. Any revision of the concept of a law of nature will bear not on the first but on the second question. Given that Hume's argument concerns itself with whether miracles, considered as unusual events, can be established as occurring, the question of whether his conception of a law of nature can be revised is irrelevant. What is at issue in his argument is not the question of how we go about explaining unusual events that have already been established as having occurred but rather the question of whether testimonial evidence can ever be sufficiently strong to establish rational belief in the occurrence of such events. The distinction between marvel and miracle and its basis in the laws of nature becomes relevant only when we grant the possibility of establishing the unusual events in the first place.

Third, if as Hume insists, our belief in the laws of nature is founded merely in a strong psychological tendency to believe in certain necessary connections and hence in the uniformity of nature, this can hardly act as a legitimate reason for rejecting reports of nonuniform events such as miracles. If the second part of the essay is any guide, Hume would be the first to admit that many people have a very strong psychological tendency to believe in miracles and hence in the nonuniformity of nature. At the level of mere psychological tendencies, there seems no reason to prefer Hume's belief in uniformity over others' belief in miracles. Only if he is prepared to argue that his tendency to believe in the uniformity of nature is somehow grounded in nature itself does it become possible for him to justify his harsh treatment of those with a tendency to believe in miracles. This, however, would be inconsistent with his explicitly stated views on induction and causality.

Wilson attempts to escape this conclusion by arguing there is good reason to prefer the belief in uniformity over belief in miracles. His argument is that belief in miracles explains nothing and leaves our experience incomprehensible, whereas belief in uniformity makes science possible. It is science alone that is capable of satisfying our curiosity and desire for truth. According to Wilson, belief in the uniformity of nature may be based on a psychological tendency, but it is rationally justified in a way that belief in miracles can never be.

This response begs the question of whether Hume's treatment of induction is consistent with the view of science being espoused by Wilson. Wilson seems to feel that any difficulty in this regard can be overcome if we realize that "the fact that we run across an event that violates a regular pattern of our experience provides evidence only that the pattern is not a law, but it does not falsify the belief that *there is* a law that explains it, for the latter can be inferred on the basis of our more general experience, which leads us to conclude that for any event there is a law that explains it." What Wilson fails to see is that any appeal to experience as justifying the conclusion that for every event there is a law that explains it is inconsistent with Hume's account of induction. Once one accepts Hume's denial of necessary connections and his reduction of causality to constant conjunction, it becomes impossible to argue that the fact that certain events have been constantly conjoined in the past provides *any* reason for thinking they will be constantly, or even probably, conjoined in the future.[6] Any appeal to the rules of eliminative induction as grounding science presupposes that we can predict the future on the basis of past experience and involves an implicit view of induction and causation that contradicts Hume's explicit treatment of these problems.[7]

A second approach taken by those sympathetic to Hume is to admit that, as it stands, his treatment of the laws of nature in his essay on miracles is inconsistent with his treatment of causality and induction but to argue that some relatively minor revisions will save his argument. Thus Antony Flew, while admitting that Hume does not justify his use of words like "infallible" or "unalterable" and that "any attempt to use our knowledge, or presumed knowledge, of ... a merely numerical universal proposition as an evidential canon by which to justify the outright rejection of any testimony to the occurrence of a falsifying exception would be a preposterous piece of question begging,"[8] has nevertheless attempted to defend him by developing the idea of physical impossibility. An event that is physically impossible is not impossible in the sense that it is inconceivable but impossible in the sense that its occurrence is not compatible with the truth of well-evidenced nomologicals. Given that we have good reason to believe that the nomologicals are true, we have good reason to deny the possibility of miracles. We can, however, admit the occurrence of what Hume calls marvels, since these are simply exceptions to merely extensional, numerically universal propositions, not to genuine laws of nature.

Promising though it might initially seem, this revision of the argument is not without problems. The nomologicals Flew has in mind are the theoretical laws employed in the various sciences, but these are a far cry from what Hume calls laws of nature. Hume is quite prepared, for example, to say that it is a law of nature that fire is extinguished by water (E 114–15), but one would search in vain in the sciences to find a nomological stating this. Flew, therefore, is quite right to point out that Hume does not distinguish between genuine nomologicals, that is, the laws of nature, and mere numerically universal propositions, and that to dismiss testimony simply because it is not compatible with the truth of a numerically universal proposition is question begging. What Flew misses, however, is that all the miracles that Hume mentions are not exceptions to genuine nomologicals but rather to numerically universal propositions. That dead men do not rise is no more a law of nature than water extinguishing fire; rather, both are regularities of nature that we try to explain.

Two points emerge. The first is that there is no special difficulty in falsifying merely numerically universal propositions on the basis of testimonial evidence. Many of us will have read that researchers have recently succeeded in transferring genes from fireflies to tobacco plants, thus producing plants that glow in the dark. This is certainly an exception to a hitherto exceptionless regularity, yet we have no difficulty in accepting this on the basis of quite modest testimonial evidence. Why, then, should we demand an extraordinary amount of evidence to convince us that a miracle, for example, the Resurrection, occurred? If it is suggested that the reason lies in the fact that the Resurrection implies violation of genuine laws of nature, but the glowing tobacco plant does not, the proper reply is that this is not at all evident. If, by intelligent manipulation of natural processes, human agents can produce an exception to an otherwise exceptionless regularity without violating the laws of nature, there seems no reason to think that a divine agent could not do likewise.[9]

Second, neither Hume nor Flew provides an adequate foundation for drawing a distinction between the merely unusual and the genuinely miraculous. Both attempt to argue that a miracle is a violation of the laws of nature but that an unusual event, a marvel, is not. In Hume's case this fails because if the laws of nature are conceived simply as hitherto exceptionless regularities, a sufficiently unusual event, no less than a miracle, would violate them. In Flew's case this fails because miracles, although exceptions to general regularities of nature, need not be conceived as violating genuine nomologicals, and thus neither miracles nor unusual events violate the laws of nature. This is not to argue that such a distinction is not important or cannot be drawn, only that Hume and Flew do not provide the basis upon which it can be made.[10]

We have seen that there are good reasons for upholding the judgement that Hume's discussion of miracles is inconsistent with his earlier treatment of induction and causality. The key question, then, is not whether he is inconsistent but how serious is his inconsistency. Does it vitiate his argument entirely, or can it be fairly easily salvaged? Two issues that bear directly on this question are whether the argument is to be conceived as an offensive or defensive weapon and whether, leaving aside the question of consistency with his earlier comments concerning induction and causality, his account of the laws of nature can be defended. If his argument is conceived as a defensive weapon, then the question of consistency will seem less worrisome, since it is then possible to think of it simply as an *ad hominem* reply designed to confute an overly ambitious opponent, not to state his own position. If his account of the laws of nature is defensible, then it may prove to be an important and worthwhile argument in its own right, even if it is inconsistent with other parts of his philosophy.

Hume's argument has traditionally been interpreted as an offensive weapon designed to show that belief in miracles could never be justified on the basis of testimonial evidence. Flew has attacked this interpretation, arguing that Hume did not conceive of it as capable of providing an insuperable bulwark against belief. Very briefly, Flew's justification of his interpretation is that Hume uses the comparatively weak word "check" to describe the effect of his argument on belief and that the traditional interpretation cannot explain why he found it necessary to include subsidiary arguments in part 2 of his discussion of miracles, since this would make no sense if he regarded the argument in part 1 as decisive.[11]

Although I do not propose to go into detail, three points, out of many that count against Flew's interpretation, are worth mentioning.[12] First, it is significant that the traditional interpretation was the one adopted in all the responses made during Hume's lifetime and that he never raised any objection to this reading of his argument. This is very hard to explain if he was convinced that his critics had fundamentally misunderstood the argument.

Second, scattered throughout part 2 are a number of comments that can only be interpreted as references to the argument of part 1 understood according to the traditional interpretation. To mention but two examples, we find him writing that "a miracle, supported by any human testimony, [is] more properly a subject of derision than of argument"(E 124) and that even if "miracles were immediately proved upon the spot, before judges of unquestioned integrity, attested by witnesses of credit and distinction, in a learned age, and on the most eminent theatre that is now in the world" we could dismiss such reports on the basis of "the absolute impossibility or miraculous nature of the events, which they relate" (E 124–5).[13]

Third, Hume's language indicates not a defensive attitude, but an aggressive certitude. The use of phrases such as "decisive," "*silence* the most arrogant bigotry and superstition," "free us from their impertinent solicitations," "everlasting check to all kinds," and "as long as the world endure" (E 110) supports the traditional reading of the argument as an offensive weapon. This reading is further confirmed by Hume's willingness to talk of the absolute impossibility of testimonial evidence ever being sufficiently strong to establish the occurrence of a miracle. He can scarcely have failed to realize that his assertion that "the proof against a miracle ... is as entire as any argument from experience can possibly be imagined ... [and that a miracle can be] rendered credible, [only] by an opposite proof which is superior" (E 114–15) implies that no testimony could ever be sufficiently strong to establish belief in a miracle.[14]

Since the traditional interpretation that the argument was intended as an offensive weapon is correct, it follows that critics who have charged that Hume cannot consistently press his argument have a point.

With regard to Hume's conception of the laws of nature, it is clear that his account cannot support his argument. Writing when he did, he can hardly be faulted for this, but he makes no distinction between genuine laws of nature and merely extensional, numerically universal propositions.[15] Neither does he show any awareness that laws of nature typically contain terms that refer not directly to observed regularities but to unobservable entities and properties. Further, he is unaware of the distinction that must be drawn between the laws of nature and the "stuff" of nature, whose behaviour they describe.[16] Contemporary attempts to defend his argument invariably involve revising his account of the laws of nature. However, as was indicated earlier and as I have argued in detail elsewhere, once a more adequate conception of the laws of nature is substituted, miracles need not be defined as violating any laws of nature.[17]

In summary, Hume's treatment of miracles is not consistent with his treatment of causality and induction. Attempts to salvage his argument by viewing it as an *ad hominem* weapon devised to confute overly ambitious theists fail to do justice to the text and the context in which it was written and discussed. Attempts to salvage it by revising his inadequate concept of a law of nature ignore the fact that once a more accurate account is substituted, there is no need to view miracles as violating the laws of nature. This suggests that not only was Hume inconsistent in pressing it but also that the argument is itself either question-begging or irrelevant.

NOTES

1 Commenting on the freezing of water, Hume writes that "Such an event ... requires a pretty strong testimony to render it credible to people in a warm climate; but still it is not miraculous." He later continues, "let us suppose that the fact which they affirm, instead of being only marvellous, is really miraculous;" David Hume *Enquiries Concerning the Human Understanding and Concerning the Principles of Morals*, ed. L.A. Selby-Bigge, 2nd ed. (1902; Oxford 1972), 114 and n. Further references ("E") will be given in the text.

2 It may be granted that Hume's general philosophy is quite consistent with the type of argument Wilson formulates. It is not, however, the argument that Hume develops in "Of Miracles."

3 It is surprising that after suggesting that a common criticism of Hume is that his discussion of miracles is inconsistent with his account of the laws of nature, the only representative of this position that Wilson discusses is C.D. Broad. Other important commentators who have taken this position, such as Flew, are ignored.

4 C.D. Broad, "Hume's Theory of the Credibility of Miracles," *Proceedings of the Aristotelian Society* n.s. 17 (1916–17): 77–94. Broad writes, "If we examined all the cases where people did come to life again and found that they had something common and peculiar to them we need not suppose a miracle. Let the common quality be *q*. Then we should merely have to modify our general law and say: All men, except those who have the quality *q*, remain dead when they are once dead. This law would have no exceptions. And the resurrection of the persons with the quality *q* would not be a miracle, but merely an instance of another general law, viz.: All men who have the quality *q* can be raised from the dead.

It must be noticed that some explanation of this kind is always theoretically possible. It is therefore true to say that no testimony, however good, will *necessitate* a belief in a miracle. It is always possible (and nearly always reasonable), even if the alleged exceptional cases be admitted, to hold that they have some common and peculiar characteristics, though this may be too minute or obscure for us to detect" (89–90). See, however, chapter 1, above, note 38.

5 It is an error, therefore, to suggest, as does J.C.A. Gaskin, *Hume's Philosophy of Religion* (London: Macmillan Press 1978), 122, that Hume can dispense with the distinction he attempts to draw between marvels and miracles.

6 Several colleagues have suggested in response to this point that Hume's account of induction and causality leaves open the possibility that our psychological makeup is such that we necessarily come to expect that events that were conjoined in the past will be conjoined in the future and that this psychological necessity provides a foundation for the scientific enterprise.

In reply, two points deserve emphasis. First, it is not clear what this psychological necessity amounts to. Second, and more importantly, even if there is such a psychological necessity, it provides no reason whatsoever for thinking that events which were constantly conjoined in the past will in fact be constantly conjoined in the future.

7 If, as Wilson insists, Hume sets high value on some such methods guiding science and achieving truth, this is further evidence that Hume is guilty of inconsistency.

8 Antony Flew, *Hume's Philosophy of Belief* (London: Routledge & Kegan Paul 1961), 122.

9 I have worked this out in this volume, chapter 3 and in *Water Into Wine?* (Montreal: McGill-Queen's University Press 1988).

Wilson wants to object to my argument on the basis that (1) the idea of a supra-sensible or non-natural cause is unintelligible and that (2) even if it were intelligible, miracles would still violate the laws of nature, since God's intervention would violate the order of natural causes, that is, the regularities governing sensible occurrences.

In the absence of any argument why the idea of a non-natural cause is unintelligible, Wilson's first objection amounts to begging the question in favour of naturalism and can be ignored. His second argument fails to recognize the relevance of the distinction I drew in my earlier article and in my book between the laws of nature and the stuff of nature whose behaviour the laws describe. It also fails to recognize that the regularities of nature, are in many instances, interrupted by our intelligent manipulation of natural processes, yet we feel no compulsion to talk of the violation of the laws of nature. If, as I argue, miracles are analogous to an agent's intelligent manipulation of natural processes, Wilson has yet to provide a reason for asserting that miracles must violate the laws of nature.

10 See chapter 8, below, and my *Water Into Wine?*

11 Antony Flew, *Hume's Philosophy*, 176–7.

12 Those wishing a fuller discussion of this issue will find R. M. Burns, *The Great Debate on Miracles* (Lewisburg, PA: Bucknell University Press 1981) chapter 7, helpful.

13 Hume's caveat "or miraculous nature" is a reference back to the distinction he wishes to draw between marvels and miracles. He is willing to allow testimonial evidence to establish marvels, but not miracles. As we have seen, however, this distinction bears not on the means by which the occurrence of unusual events is to be established but on the question of how unusual events are to be explained. It cannot, therefore, help Hume in the present context. Either a body of testimonial evidence is sufficient to establish the occurrence of an unusual event, or it is not. The question of whether an event can be given a naturalistic explanation or not is separate and logically independent from the question of whether its occurrence can be established.

14 Many commentators customarily treat these remarks as a mere slip or carelessness on Hume's part, but there seems no reason, other than the desire to view him in the best possible light, to think that he did not mean to say what he said.

15 Flew, *Hume's Philosophy* 204–6.

16 See chapter 3, below.

17 See chapter 3, below, and my *Water Into Wine?*

3 Miracles and the Laws of Nature

ROBERT LARMER

In discussing the relation between miracles and the laws of nature, it is essential to make clear the meaning of the terms "miracle" and "law of nature," since both terms may be used in several different ways. I wish to begin, therefore, by briefly indicating how I use these terms. I shall then be in a position to discuss the relation between these particular concepts of miracles and the laws of nature.

I use the term "miracle" to designate an objective event that is specially caused by God: it is an event that nature would not have produced had not God intervened to bring it about. Thus, although this sense of the term "miracle" "includes the idea that wonder is called for as at least part of the appropriate response, the crux as well as the ground for the wonder is that a miracle should consist in an overriding of the order of nature."[1]

The term "law of nature" I shall take as logically equivalent to "a scientific law that is, in fact, true." I hasten to add that by scientific law I do not mean "inductive generalization" or "experimental law." Rather, I am referring to theoretical laws or principles that serve to explain the experimental laws discovered by scientists. What this means is that while the term "law of nature" refers to a universal conditional that may, in principle, be either confirmed or disconfirmed by empirical evidence, the conditional will contain terms that refer, not directly to observed regularities, but to unobservable entities and properties, electrons, for example, that serve to explain observed regularities. Laws of nature, therefore, cannot be confirmed or disconfirmed directly by observation; they must be confirmed or disconfirmed indirectly through predictions made on the basis of these laws.

My view of the relation between miracles and natural laws is this. Miracles considered as objective events specially caused by God can conceivably occur in a world that behaves, always and everywhere, completely in accordance with the laws of nature. Such a view is, obviously, a controversial one. It is usually thought that if one defines the terms "miracle" and "law of nature" in the way I have defined them, then one is committed to the proposition "If a miracle occurs then some law of nature has been violated." The reasoning behind this seems to be that a miracle in the objective sense must constitute an overriding of nature but that such an overriding can take place only if one or more laws of nature are violated. Such reasoning, however, is fallacious. I shall show that it is quite conceivable that an overriding of nature could take place without any law of nature being violated.

In order to see this, let us begin by examining some commonplace features of the "covering law theory of explanation." In such a theory the typical form an explanation takes is

$C_1 \dots C_n$
$L_1 \dots L_m$
Therefore E,

where $C_1 \dots C_n$ is a set of singular statements describing relevant initial conditions, where $L_1 \dots L_m$ is a set of general laws, and where E, the event to be explained, is a logical consequence of the conjunction of the Cs and Ls, but not of the Cs alone.[2] As is well known, this same scheme can be used to predict the occurrence of E if $C_1 \dots C_n$ occur.

Now, although we may often speak as though the laws of nature are, in themselves, sufficient to explain the occurrence of an event, this is not really so. Clearly, the laws of nature, inasmuch as they are merely conditionals, cannot, by themselves, explain the actual occurrence of an event. A scientific explanation must make reference not only to the laws of nature, but also to initial conditions, to the actual "stuff" of nature, the matter or, more accurately, mass/energy whose behaviour is described by the laws of nature.

If we keep in mind this basic distinction between laws of nature and the initial conditions, it can be seen that although a miracle is an event that never would have occurred had not nature been overridden and although the notion of a miracle is logically dependent upon the notion of a known order to which it constitutes an exception, this in no way entails the claim that a miracle involves a violation of, suspension of, or exception to, the laws of nature. If God creates or annihilates a unit of mass/energy, he does change the material conditions to which the laws of nature apply. He thereby produces an event that nature on its own would not have produced, a miracle, in short, but he breaks no law of nature.

It is important to emphasize that such an event in no way implies that the laws of nature are violated, suspended, or even have exceptions. One does not, for example, contravene the laws of motion if one tosses an extra ball into a group of balls in motion on a billiard table. There is no moment of time at which the laws of motion are contravened. What one does is to change the material conditions to which the laws of motion apply, and hence one changes the result that would otherwise have been expected. Similarly, God, by creating or annihilating a unit or units of mass/energy, may produce in nature an event that would not otherwise have been expected without violating, suspending, or creating exceptions to the laws of nature.

Thus, it will not do to argue that if a miracle occurs then some implication of the complete set of the laws of nature is contravened, and, therefore, by *modus tollens*, at least one of the laws in the set is contravened. Put somewhat differently, it will not do to argue that if a miracle is an exception to the regular course of nature, then it is *ipso facto* an exception to some law, since the complete set of laws entails a complete description of the course of nature.[3] What such an argument fails to take into account is the fact that the complete set of laws entails the complete description of the course of nature only if the material conditions to which the laws apply are not changed. Thus, to revert to our billiard table example, the laws of motion entail the description of the actions of the billiard balls only so long as no extra balls are introduced into the system. Similarly, the complete set of the laws of nature entails a complete description of the course of nature only so long as God does not create or annihilate mass/energy, thus changing the material conditions to which the laws apply.

There are two major objections that might be raised against this argument. The first is that such a conclusion can be reached only by offering an arbitrary, unrealistic definition of the term "law of nature." The second is that even if it is granted that the definition of "law of nature" is adequate, the argument still implies that at least one law of nature must be violated if a miracle occurs, since the creation or annihilation of mass/energy implies that the first law of thermodynamics (the principle of the conservation of energy) has been violated.[4]

Considering the first objection, it might, I suppose, be urged by a critic that the term "law of nature" is best understood as meaning merely a well-established regularity of nature. Thus, for example, the critic might maintain that it is a law of nature that virgins do not give birth. Presumably, if the miracle of the Virgin Birth actually occurred, the law of nature that virgins do not give birth must have been violated.

If one grants the critic this definition, then it seems to follow that a miracle is indeed a violation of the laws of nature. Unfortunately for the critic, it also follows that a number of non-miraculous events that we are not normally inclined to view as being violations of the laws of nature must be classed as violations of these laws. Consider, for example, the possible case of a virgin who, through surgical procedures, has a fertilized egg implanted in her uterus. After a period of nine months this woman gives birth. The point, obviously, is that, although we might find such an event unusual and newsworthy, we would scarcely be inclined to view it as violating the laws of nature. Given that we know the relevant set of conditions, regularities in nature, such as the fact that virgins do not in the normal course of events give birth, are explicable by reference to the laws of nature; it does not seem plausible to view them as being themselves laws of nature.

The critic might, of course, argue that this distinction does not fully resolve the difficulty. Granted that we must distinguish between laws of nature and well-established regularities, we are nevertheless firmly convinced that there are a great number of well-established regularities of nature that, in the absence of extraordinary circumstances, admit of no exceptions. Surely, it might be urged, the regularity that in the normal course of events, virgins do not give birth admits of no exceptions.

The claim that we are firmly, and probably justifiably, convinced that, all other things being equal, some regularities of nature admit of no exceptions, must be granted. It must also be granted that our conviction that virgins do not, in the usual course of events, give birth, falls into this category. The believer in the occurrence of a miracle contends however, that all other things were not equal. Thus, for example, those who believe in the Virgin Birth would hold that this miracle is, in some respects, analogous to the hypothetical case of the virgin, who, through surgical procedures, has a fertilized egg implanted in her uterus. The two cases are analogous, not in the means by which the result of a virgin birth is achieved, but in that in neither case are "all other things equal." In our hypothetical case, a human agent, that is, the surgeon, intervenes, changes a material situation to which the laws of nature apply and produces in nature an event that would not otherwise occur and that constitutes an exception to a well-established regularity of nature. In the case of the Virgin Birth, a divine agent, that is, God, intervenes, changes the material situation to which the laws of nature apply, and produces in nature an event that would not otherwise occur and that constitutes an exception to a well-established regularity of nature. In neither case are "all other things equal," and in neither case is there any reason to suppose that the laws of nature were violated, suspended, or suffered an exception.[5]

My argument, then, is that miracles are, in an important sense, analogous to acts of human agents. Thus, if a human agent may act in such a way as to produce an exception to a regularity of nature that in the absence of action on the part of some agent would admit of no exception, it seems reasonable to suppose that a divine agent may act similarly. It follows, therefore, that if a human agent need not violate any law of nature in producing an event that is an exception to a well-established regularity of nature, then neither need a divine agent violate any law of nature in producing such an event.

The critic might at this point reply that I have not made miracles easier to conceive so much as raised problems concerning the notion of agency. If that notion implies that agents in some significant way stand outside physical processes yet act in such a way as to influence physical processes, this suggests that some form of interactionist dualism is a correct theory of the mind-body relation. Surely, however, such a theory is difficult to defend.

Such a criticism suggests, correctly I think, that in the final analysis the question of miracles cannot be considered in isolation from a number of other important philosophical issues. I do not, in this paper, propose to explore further the notion of agency and its relation to the question of miracles and the mind-body problem. It is appropriate to note, however, that even if the notion of agency I have employed implies the truth of some version of interactionist dualism, it is not usually objected that the interaction of mind and body implies that natural laws are violated.[6]

Prima facie, the second objection seems much harder to deal with than the first. There seems no way around the conclusion that if a miracle involves either the creation or annihilation of mass/energy, then its occurrence implies that the principle of the conservation of energy has been violated. I hope to show that this difficulty is apparent rather than real. I shall do this by distinguishing between the principle of the conservation of energy considered as a scientific law and the principle of the conservation of energy considered as a metaphysical principle. I shall argue that the occurrence of a miracle would not call into question the truth of the principle considered as a scientific law, but it would call into question the truth of the principle considered as a metaphysical principle.

The principle of the conservation of energy is commonly stated as "Energy can neither be created nor destroyed although its form may change" or as "In an isolated system the total amount of energy remains constant although its form may change." Usually the two formulations are used interchangeably, the unspoken assumption being that they are logically equivalent. A moment's thought, however, reveals they are not. One can deduce from the statement "Energy can neither be created nor destroyed" the statement "In an isolated system the total amount of energy remains constant," but one cannot from the statement "In an isolated system energy remains constant," deduce the statement "Energy can neither be created nor destroyed."

What this reveals is that the statement "Energy can neither be created nor destroyed" is considerably stronger than the statement "In an isolated system the total amount of energy remains constant." The former statement could not, for example, be held by a theist, since such a statement by definition rules out the possibility of creation of energy *ex nihilo*. By contrast, a theist could affirm the second statement that "In an isolated system the total amount of energy remains constant," since such a statement implies nothing concerning the possibility of creation *ex nihilo*, just as it implies nothing concerning whether, in fact, the physical universe is an isolated system or open to the causal influence of God. The first statement of the principle of the conservation of energy is thus much stronger than the second in that it proves to be a defining postulate of physicalism, whereas the second statement does not.

The relevance of the distinction is this. The person who believes in the occurrence of miracles is under no compulsion to deny the weak form of the principle of the conservation of energy, that is, the well-evidenced claim that in a causally isolated system energy remains constant. He rejects the much weaker claim that nature is an isolated system in the sense that it is not open to the causal influence of God. He is, therefore, in a position to accept all scientific claims that suggest that in an isolated system, energy remains constant. He is, in short, in a position to accept the principle of the conservation of energy when it is formulated as a scientific law and not as a defining postulate of physicalism.

He must, of course, deny the strong form of the principle of the conservation of energy. In doing this, however, he does not deny that it is a law of nature that in an isolated system energy is conserved. Neither, it must be emphasized, does he maintain that this law of nature is in any way contravened in the case of a miracle. He denies only that energy can neither be created nor destroyed, only the physicalist's assertion that there exists nothing other than nature by which energy could be created or destroyed.

Now it certainly must be admitted that the statement "Energy cannot be created or destroyed" is one that seems to many people to be obviously true; so much so that it is often confused with the well-evidenced but much weaker claim that "The total energy of an isolated system remains constant." The source of this confusion may lie in the fact that it is often at least an implicit assumption of many thinkers that nature exists and functions, so to speak, "on its own"; that nature is all that exists and is, therefore, not open to addition or subtraction by something external to it. Once this assumption has been made, the claim that "Energy cannot be created or destroyed" is bound to seem very plausible.[7] In the case of reports of miracles, however, precisely this assumption is being questioned, and to object to such reports on the basis that the occurrence of miracles would not be consistent with the truth of the claim that "Energy can neither be created nor destroyed" is only to beg the question of the truth of physicalism.

The conclusion is clear. Insofar as the principle of the conservation of energy is formulated as a scientific law, a miracle constitutes no violation of it. One may agree that "If a system is isolated then its total energy remains constant" without, thereby, agreeing that nature is in fact an isolated system. Insofar as the principle of the conservation of energy is formulated as a metaphysical principle it, by definition, rules out the possibility of a miracle. This should come as no surprise, since so formulated it constitutes a defining postulate of physicalism and hence, by definition, also rules out theism and the idea of creation *ex nihilo*.

The claim that a miracle occurred would conflict, therefore, not with the well-evidenced scientific claim that the total energy of an isolated system remains constant, but with the metaphysical claim that nature is an isolated system not open to the action of God. I conclude that insofar as the principle of the conservation of energy is asserted as a law of nature and not as a somewhat disguised metaphysical claim, a miracle need not be conceived as being a violation of, suspension of, or exception to, it. Thus, the idea that a miracle must be an event that nature would not produce on its own and that constitutes an exception to the regular course of nature does not entail the conclusion that a miracle must contravene the laws of nature.

This conclusion follows, of course, only if it is appropriate to view a miracle as an event that is at least partially caused by an act of creation or annihilation of mass/energy by a rational agent who transcends nature. I use the phrase "at least partially" because it seems clear that an event that is termed a miracle may be a product of both the already functioning processes of nature and an act of creation or annihilation. Thus, for example, the miracle of the Virgin Birth can be seen as an event in which an act of creation by God (the creation of a spermatozoon in the body of Mary) combined with existent natural processes (the normal growth and development of a foetus during pregnancy) to produce the miraculous event we call the Virgin Birth. Or, to develop a different example in which the annihilation of mass/ energy may have played a part, certain acts of healing on Christ's part may have involved annihilation of material making up harmful tumours or infections. Or, to take this line of thought a step further, it is entirely possible that a miracle may involve both acts of creation and acts of annihilation. Christ's healing of lepers might, for example, have involved both the annihilation of diseased cells and the creation of new tissue to replace tissue previously lost to the disease. In all of these examples, it seems quite clear that an act of creation or annihilation may combine with already functioning natural processes to produce an event we would term a miracle. On the other hand, it should be emphasized, a miracle need not have any natural processes linked to it; the miracle of the multiplication of the loaves and fishes seems to have been a direct act of creation in which already functioning natural processes played little part.

Miracles, therefore, need not involve any violation of, suspension of, or exceptions to the laws of nature. Rather, they involve acts of creation or annihilation of the initial conditions to which the laws apply. It is clear that God, by annihilating or creating mass/energy and so changing the material conditions to which the laws of nature apply, could produce within nature events that nature would not otherwise produce, without thereby violating, suspending, or creating exceptions to, any of the laws of nature.

This conclusion is a significant one. Since Hume, a major objection to the claim that there could be a rationally justified belief in the occurrence of miracles has been that the historical evidence seeming to favour such events must inevitably conflict with the scientific evidence, which supports belief in the laws of nature. Clearly, however, if a miracle need not be considered a violation of the laws of nature, there is no reason to believe that the two bodies of evidence conflict. Since it is a fundamental principle in assessing evidence to accept as much evidence as is possible and yet develop a coherent account, it seems entirely possible that historical evidence might justify belief in the occurrence of miracles. It is, therefore, quite conceivable that belief in miracles may be justified on historical grounds.

NOTES

1 Antony Flew, "Miracles," *The Encyclopedia of Philosophy* (1967), 5:346.
2 Jaegwon Kim, "Explanation in Science," *The Encyclopedia of Philosophy* (1967), 3:159.
3 I am assuming for the sake of argument that the laws of nature are absolute and not statistical, and that the working of physical processes is deterministic. My aim is to show that even granting this, miracles need not be conceived as being violations of the laws of nature.
4 Since mass is thought to be a form of energy, we may speak of the principle of the conservation of energy rather than the principle of the conservation of mass/energy. For the sake of convenience, I will refer merely to the principle of the conservation of energy.
5 See, for example, C. S. Lewis, *Miracles, A Preliminary Study* (New York: Macmillan 1947; report, Glasgow: Fontana 1960), 62–3.
6 It is sometimes objected that the interaction of mind and body would violate the first law of thermodynamics. This is not the case, however, as I shall show in the remaining part of my essay. So long as one opts for the "scientific form" of the first law of thermodynamics, the interaction of mind and body need not be conceived as violating the first law.
7 It becomes plausible because on this view there is nothing either to create or to destroy energy.

4 Against Miracles

JOHN COLLIER

Robert Larmer argues (this volume, chap. 3) that even if all physical events are subject to deterministic natural laws, miracles can
occur. He concludes that the Humean argument that belief in
miracles cannot be rationally justified – because belief that a miracle has occurred must inevitably conflict with belief in the laws
of nature – is fallacious, since the occurrence of miracles need
not violate the laws of nature.

There are two problems with Larmer's argument. The first,
which I will deal with only briefly, concerns Larmer's conclusion.
Natural laws conceived (as Larmer does) as explanatory principles
rather than observational generalizations do not enter into
Hume's argument in any essential way. John Wright argues con-
vincingly that Hume believed we can have no rational evidence
for causal relations, merely for the regularities that he called
"natural laws."[1] It would contradict Hume's sceptical philosophy
to conclude that he identified causation with these regularities.
Natural laws, therefore, can enter into a Humean argument
against miracles only as observational generalizations. This interpretation is supported by the fact that Hume makes no mention of causation in his chapter "Of Miracles" in the *Enquiry*,
except to say that contrary evidence can cause doubt or
uncertainty.[2]

Hume's argument against the rationality of belief in miracles does not prove that miracles are impossible but merely that the evidence in their favour will always be less than the evidence against them. One characteristic of miracles, or, more correctly, of reported miraculous events, is that they are highly unusual, which implies that we have abundant contrary evidence that events of that sort do not happen. This evidence undermines any evidence that a particular miraculous event has occurred. The existence of miracles is not, however, inconsistent with the impossibility of there being a balance of evidence in their favour.

Hume's argument cuts against the rationality of belief that unusual natural events have occurred just as much as it cuts against the rationality of belief in particular miracles. The difference is that unusual natural events, unlike miracles, can be explained and justified, at least potentially, by hitherto unknown natural laws (see Hume's example of the Indian prince, E 113–14). Belief in miracles could not receive this more refined support from natural laws. Hume's argument would have no force against fairly commonplace miracles but commonplace miracles are not at issue. Whatever one thinks of the Humean argument, Larmer's proposed compatibility of miracles with natural laws raises a separate issue.

The second problem is Larmer's argument that miracles are compatible with natural laws. If this could be established, it would be interesting independently of the Humean argument. One could, perhaps, justify belief in miracles on the basis of some supernatural or divine laws grounded in theological rather than scientific explanation. If natural laws conflict with miracles, then science would defeat any attempt at such a justification due to the strength of the evidence for the laws of science, but if there is no conflict, the field is open for theological explanation. Fortunately, we are saved from considerable difficult work, since Larmer's argument fails.

Larmer distinguishes the action of natural laws from the material circumstances to which they apply. He argues that natural laws are conditionals, the conditions for which must be satisfied by the stuff of nature. God, he says, could alter the stuff of nature, thereby overriding nature without violating the laws, just the conditions. This is analogous, he argues, to the way we can introduce an extra billiard ball to a group on a table without violating the laws governing the motion of the balls on the table. The new addition merely changes the circumstances under which the laws apply.

Larmer's argument is restricted to the deterministic case of a universe that obeys Newton's laws and classical thermodynamics. To the obvious objection that the introduction of an event into the universe violates the first law of thermodynamics (the principle of the conservation of energy), Larmer replies that the law applies to isolated systems. If we assume that the physical universe is an isolated system, then God could not introduce new matter/energy into the universe. This assumption, though, begs the question of the possibility of God's miraculous activity. If God adds an event not normally found in the world, he changes the conditions of the world so that it is not an isolated system, but His activity, Larmer argues, does not violate the first law in its conditional form.

Larmer misrepresents the first law. It applies specifically to physically isolated systems, namely, ones into which neither energy nor matter flows from the outside. Either the world is a physically isolated system, in which case God's introduction of matter would violate the conditions of the first law, or else it is not, in which case the conditions of the first law require that either God or some part of God or else some otherworldly realm under God's control is physical and thus subject to physical law. If something is supernatural merely because it is caused by God, then the usual assumption that God created the physical world would make all natural laws supernatural, which is contradictory. Larmer might, however, accept that miracles are entirely physical phenomena but are still distinguished from natural events by not having a complete explanation in terms of natural laws.

The impossibility of a complete explanation in terms of natural laws is not itself sufficient for an event to be a miracle, as the fundamental indeterminacy postulated by the standard interpretation of quantum theory shows. In any case, Larmer asserts that his argument applies to classical worlds. If so, the attempt to distinguish miraculous events in terms of the impossibility of a complete naturalistic explanation falls afoul of Laplacean determinacy. The determinacy of Newton's laws requires that conditions at any time in the physical world determine all past and future states. If God were to intervene physically in the world, His actions could be explained by Newton's laws in light of the effects of these actions, just as we can explain the effects of a meteorite hitting the Earth in terms of prior physical conditions existing somewhere else. God's action, if compatible with Newton's laws, would be no more miraculous than the action of a stray meteorite wandering in from a hitherto unknown part of the physical world.

There is a general argument available that shows that supernatural action on the world must violate physical law. Newton proposed that absolute space acts on the world to produce the inertial effects observed during accelerated motion but is not affected itself by this action. Ernst Mach observed that this violates Newton's own principle that for every action there is an equal and opposite reaction.[3] The notion of an unmoved mover is inherently contrary to the law of reaction, which contemporary physics does not reject. Even a spontaneous appearance of matter due to fluctuations in the quantum field would change that field. To the extent that God acts on a world in which physical law is not violated, His action is explainable just as much as any other physical activity: there is no room for miracles without violating physical law.

NOTES

1 John P. Wright, *The Sceptical Realism of David Hume* (Minneapolis, MN: University of Minnesota Press 1983), 125–35.
2 David Hume, *Enquiries Concerning Human Understanding and Concerning the Principles of Morals*, ed. L.A. Selby-Bigge, 2nd ed. (1902; Oxford 1972), 112. Further references ("E") will be given in the text.
3 I am grateful to Herb Korte for pointing this out to me.

5 Against "Against Miracles"

ROBERT LARMER

In chapter 4 John Collier attempts to refute the claim I made in chapter 3 that miracles can conceivably occur in a world that behaves completely in accordance with the laws of nature. I wish, briefly, to give my reasons for thinking he fails.

His first objection seems to be that I have misunderstood Hume's argument. I find this criticism puzzling, since I do not mention Hume until the last paragraph of chapter 3 and then only to say that "since Hume, a major objection to the claim that there could be a rationally justified belief in the occurrence of miracles has been that the historical evidence seeming to favour such events must inevitably conflict with the scientific evidence, which supports belief in the laws of nature." Since I nowhere discuss Hume's famous argument in chapter 3, it seems premature to charge me with misinterpreting it. However, since it is my presumed misunderstanding of Hume that provides Collier with one of the two reasons he gives for rejecting my claim, it is appropriate to make a few remarks about the relation of my argument to that of Hume.

Collier is quite right to point out that what I mean by the term "law of nature" is something quite different from what Hume meant by this term. I think that the laws of nature are explanatory principles; Hume thought that they are simply well-established regularities of nature. Collier neglects to mention two important facts, however.

The first is that in my article I consider the view that the term "law of nature" is best understood as meaning simply a well-established regularity of nature and that I give reasons for rejecting this view. My basic argument is that it forces us to define as violations a number of non-miraculous events we are not normally inclined to regard as violations of the laws of nature. For example, as I mentioned in chapter 2, researchers have recently succeeded in transferring genes from fireflies to tobacco plants, thus producing plants that glow in the dark. If the Humean view that a law of nature is simply a well-established regularity is correct, then it follows that a law of nature was violated the first time one of these plants glowed in the dark, since we had a uniform experience prior to that event that tobacco plants do not glow in the dark. My point, of course, is that we do not think that events like this really are violations of the laws of nature. It follows, therefore, that we cannot define a law of nature simply as a well-established regularity of nature.

The second thing Collier neglects to mention is that I am not alone in rejecting Hume's account of natural law but that even the staunchest proponents of Hume's argument assert that it must be revised. Antony Flew is explicit on this point, arguing that "the lack of an adequate conception of a law of nature would make it impossible for Hume ... to justify a distinction between the marvellous or the unusual and the truly miraculous, and ... prevented him from exploiting to the full his own distinctive conception of the opposition of proofs."[1] Although he defends the essential validity of Hume's argument, Flew insists that its defence must involve a revision of Hume's definition of natural law, since "to dismiss out of hand all testimony to the occurrence beyond the range of our observations of a counterexample on the sole ground that such an occurrence would falsify the universal generalization based upon our observations to date would be arbitrary and bigoted."[2]

Before I move on to Collier's second criticism of my argument, I want to comment on two further remarks he makes concerning Hume. I agree with him that Hume did not attempt to prove that miracles are impossible.[3] Hume's argument is considerably more subtle: its conclusion is not that miracles cannot occur but that belief in miracles can never be justified on the basis of testimonial evidence. I also agree that Hume's strategy was to argue that since miracles are unusual events, the abundant evidence that events of that sort do not occur undermines any testimonial evidence that a particular miracle has occurred.

Where I part company with Collier is over the legitimacy of Hume's reasoning. I think Hume commits the fallacy of division in reasoning in this manner.[4] From the mere fact that one class contains a great many more members than another, we can conclude very little. No theist would want to say that the class of events properly called miracles approaches the size of the class of non-miraculous events, but that does not mean that the probability that any particular miracle occurred is low. The existential status of a conceivable event cannot be determined simply by considering the numerical size of the class to which it belongs. Rather, it must be determined by considering all relevant evidence. Any attempt to argue otherwise rules out not only miracles but any number of well-established, but nevertheless rare, events. To revert to my previous example, it is a rare event for a tobacco plant to glow in the dark and I have certainly never witnessed such an event, yet the testimonial evidence justifies me in believing that the probability that such an event actually occurred is very high. The fact that an event does not commonly occur can scarcely be considered evidence that it never occurs. If Hume's argument is to be defended it cannot be on the basis that miracles are unusual events but rather on the basis that they are events that violate the laws of nature defined in a non-Humean way.

Collier comes close to realizing the difficulties inherent in Hume's argument when he remarks that it seems to undermine not just the rationality of belief in miracles but belief in any unusual event. He attempts to resolve this problem by suggesting "that unusual natural events ... can at least potentially be explained by hitherto unknown natural laws ... [but] belief in miracles could not receive this more refined support from natural laws."

His suggestion misses the point, however. What is at issue is not whether we can eventually explain an unusual event by

reference to presently unknown natural laws but whether
Hume's argument permits us to establish its occurrence in the
first place. The suggestion that we may someday be able to explain unusual events in naturalistic terms assumes precisely what
Hume's argument denies, namely, that the occurrence of singular
events can be justified on the basis of testimonial evidence, since
otherwise we would have no reason to think there is anything
that needs explanation or investigation.

Collier's second criticism of my argument is that I misrepresent
the first law of thermodynamics. He does not explain how I have
misrepresented it, but he does offer his own positive account
of it. He writes that the first law applies to physically isolated
systems, these being defined as ones into which neither energy
nor matter flows from the outside. He claims that this implies
that "either the world is a physically isolated system, in which
case God's introduction of matter would violate the conditions
of the first law, or else it is not, in which case the conditions
of the first law require that either God or some part of God
or else some otherworldly realm under God's control is physical
and thus subject to physical law."

By way of reply to this criticism, I will briefly review my account of the first law and then consider Collier's understanding
of it. In my article, I noted an ambiguity in the formulation of
the first law. It is generally stated either as "Energy can neither
be created nor destroyed" or as "In an isolated system the total
amount of energy remains constant," the unspoken assumption
being that these statements are logically equivalent. I pointed
out that they are not, since the first implies the second but the
second does not imply the first. I also pointed out that the theist
can accept the weaker scientific form of the first law, since she
denies not that energy is conserved in an isolated system but
that nature is an isolated system in the sense that it is not open
to the causal influence of God.

Collier's account of the first law falls prey to the ambiguity
I have just pointed out. He writes that the first law applies to
physically isolated systems. Scientists, however, do not talk of
physically isolated systems but simply of isolated systems, an isolated system being understood as one that is not causally affected
by something other than itself.[5] More seriously, Collier defines

an isolated system as one into which neither energy nor matter flows. The problem here is that this definition simply assumes the truth of the strong form of the first law. Unless we assume that energy can neither be created nor destroyed, there is no reason to think that a system into which neither energy nor matter has flowed is causally isolated. If God created energy within a system, we would have a system into which neither matter nor energy had flowed (that is, there would have been no transfer or movement of previously existing matter or energy from one system to another) but which could not accurately be described as isolated. Such an event would violate the strong form of the first law but not the weak form. This is precisely the point I made in my article, and I do not think Collier has provided any reason for rejecting it.

In his final paragraph, Collier gives a general argument designed to show that God cannot act on the world without violating the laws of nature. His argument is very simple. It is that the "the notion of an unmoved mover is inherently contrary to the law of reaction, which contemporary physics does not reject." Thus, whatever one may think of my arguments concerning the conservation of energy, God's action on the world must violate Newton's third law of motion.

What Collier ignores in pressing this objection is that Newton's third law refers to the relation between two physical objects. However, God is not a physical object, and the relation between God and that which He creates or annihilates is not a physical relation. It makes no sense, therefore, to suggest that God's creation or annihilation of energy is inconsistent with Newton's third law.

What is true is that any new physical objects God creates will both act upon and be acted upon by previously existing physical objects. This, however, implies no violation of the third law. Lest Collier protest that I have made life easy for myself by considering only cases of creation, let me point out that the third law concerns the *relation* between two physical objects. If, due to God annihilating it, one of these objects no longer exists, there can be no physical relation between it and the other object, and thus there can be no question of the third law being violated. Collier fails, therefore, to show that my account of miracles implies any violation of the laws of nature.

NOTES

1 Antony Flew, *Hume's Philosophy of Belief* (London: Routledge & Kegan Paul 1961), 204.
2 Ibid., 205.
3 At least this is Hume's official position. Several writers have pointed out that his later comments and use of language throw doubt on the sincerity of his earlier stated intentions. My own view is that Hume was willing to grant that miracles could conceivably occur – though he did not for a moment think they actually did – but felt that there could never, even in principle, be enough evidence to justify rational belief in their occurrence.
4 Gary Colwell, "On Defining Away The Miraculous," *Philosophy* 57 (1982):332.
5 This should come as no surprise, since there are strong links between conservation principles and causal principles. What Collier wants to call a "physically isolated" system would be one that was not casually affected by something other than itself. By introducing the term *physical*, Collier smuggles in the notion that all causes are physical ones and that changes in a system can only be caused by the flow of energy from, or into, some other physical system. This is to beg the important question of whether all causes are physical causes, however.

A good assessment of the relation between causal principles and conservation principles is Ernst Mach's *History and Root of the Principle of the Conservation of Energy*, translated and annotated by Philip E.B. Jourdain, 2d ed. (Chicago: Open Court Publishing Co. 1911).

6 Miracles and Conservation Laws

NEIL W. MacGILL

In his book *Water into Wine?*, Robert Larmer argues that miracles, even defined as involving changes in the normal course of events in the universe caused by transcendent agents, do not, or at least do not necessarily, involve events that violate the true laws of nature.[1]

In making this claim, he points out the distinction that is often drawn in the explanation of a particular event between the relevant laws of nature and the statement of the initial conditions, of the "actual stuff of nature," as he puts it, that must be true if the laws are to apply to the particular case.

If we keep in mind this basic distinction between the laws of nature and the "stuff" whose behaviour they describe [he goes on], we can see that, although a miracle is an event which never would have occurred had not nature been overridden, and although the notion of a miracle is logically dependent upon the notion of a known order to which it constitutes an exception, this in no way entails that a miracle must violate the laws of nature ... If God creates or annihilates a unit or units of mass/energy He breaks no law of nature, but He does ... change the material conditions to which the laws of nature apply. He would thereby produce an event which nature on its own would not have produced. (20)

Larmer illustrates this argument by pointing out that "We do not, for example, violate the laws of motion if we toss an extra billiard ball into a group of billiard balls in motion on a billiard table."

It is not clear at the outset whether Larmer wishes to claim that miracles *do not* violate the laws of nature or only that it is *possible* that they do not. For example, he says that he "will argue that it is *entirely conceivable* that miracles can occur in a world which behaves, always and everywhere, completely in accordance with the laws of nature." But he immediately goes on to say that "Establishing this will allow me ... to dismiss as irrelevant the question of whether it makes sense to talk of violations of laws of nature" (18). But surely this question is only irrelevant if it is shown either that miracles *do not* in fact violate the laws of nature or that if they did occur they *would not* violate them.

I do not think that Larmer does prove that miracles *cannot* violate the laws of nature, and it follows that it is very important, given his position, to show how it might be established that miracles *do in fact* occur in the way he describes, that is by the creation or annihilation of mass/energy. And yet when he comes to discuss, in chapter seven of *Water into Wine?*, the types of evidence that are relevant to establishing the occurrence of a miracle, Larmer does not mention the need to show that, at the very least, changes in the amount of mass/energy are involved.

Let us return to Larmer's argument. He goes on to point out that it might seem that the creation or annihilation of mass/energy violates one law of nature, namely, the principle of the conservation of energy. However, he argues that one must distinguish between two forms of this principle: first, the claim that "energy can neither be created nor destroyed, although its form may change"; and second, the claim that "in an isolated system the total amount of energy remains constant, although its form may change" (24).

Miracles, if they are as Larmer describes them, do not violate the second form of the principle of the conservation of energy, since when they do occur the system in which they occur is to that extent not isolated. On the other hand he agrees that they do violate the first form, since they do involve, specifically, the creation or annihilation of mass/energy.

However, Larmer claims that this first form of the principle in fact functions as a "defining postulate of physicalism" (61). It is stronger than the second form, in the sense that it entails, but is not entailed by, the second form, but, he claims, there is and can be no additional body of evidence beyond that which confirms the weaker second form that would confirm the stronger first form as the correct "deep structural assumption" that will explain the truth of the second form, which it entails (chap. 5, passim).

On the other hand, Larmer argues, if his account of miracles is correct, miracles would constitute counterinstances that would *disconfirm* the first form of the principle and show that some other deep structural assumption must be sought to explain the weaker second form (70–72).

The far-reaching significance of Larmer's suggestion about miracles begins to emerge in chapter 3 of *Water into Wine?* when he turns to a consideration of Hume's argument in the essay "On Miracles" (see also this volume, chap. 2). While he criticizes Hume in some detail, his concluding thrust is that once it is recognized that miracles need not violate any law of nature, the evidence in favour of miracles need not be balanced, as Hume argues, against the more extensive evidence in favour of the laws of nature, since both can be accepted without mutual inconsistency.

In chapter four of his book Larmer examines some arguments by modern analytical philosophers against miracles. Here again he suggests that the distinction between violations of laws of nature and changes in the conditions to which they apply is helpful in meeting some of these arguments, but he also makes use of the distinction between these "scientific" explanations, framed in terms of general laws applied to initial conditions, and "personal" explanations, framed in terms of the purposes and intentions of an agent (48). Only in the former case does explanation imply prediction, since prediction depends upon extrapolating regularities entailed by general laws, while personal, or agent, causation need not display any regularity.

Since miracles are by definition caused by an agent, their explanation does not involve, prima facie, the discovery of any underlying regularity, and as Larmer points out, "it is a controversial issue whether explanations involving references to agents can be reduced to scientific explanations" (48).

Larmer's claim that miracles do not violate laws of nature but are, rather, changes in the quantity of mass/energy and his claim that they are to be explained by agent causation rather than by "scientific" explanation are brought together in the proposal in chapter six that "a theistic worldview maintains the reality of the material world" and hence accepts the *scientific* explanation of isolated physical systems, while at the same time asserting "that the world ... was created by God and is subject to His influence" (85). Thus the correct deep structural assumption is not that energy cannot be created or destroyed but that the conservation of energy in accordance with the laws of nature in isolated systems and its occasional miraculous creation or annihilation are both to be explained by the purposes and intentions of God.

On this account, physicalism is preserved or, rather, "swallowed up" (93) as a part of a theistic worldview just because the miraculous interventions by God leave the laws of nature inviolate. Larmer sees his claim that God intervenes in nature only by creating or annihilating energy as crucial because any other form of divine intervention would be in direct conflict with His own intentions in establishing the laws of nature.

However, I think that conservation laws play a more fundamental role in scientific explanation than Larmer seems to allow. It is central to the theistic worldview he advocates that scientific laws can remain inviolate and unchallenged even if the stuff to which they apply varies in quantity as it is created or annihilated by God. But the stuff to which the laws apply does not consist in good, solid, middle-sized things like billiard balls, which are merely figments of our curious perceptual apparatus; rather, the stuff consists in theoretical entities such as mass/energy that can be understood only in virtue of their role in the scientific laws in which their names and descriptions occur. And an essential feature in the testing and hence the truth and the very meaning of such laws is that the stuff to which they refer must remain constant in quantity, that is, it must satisfy an appropriate conservation law. If this conservation law is found to be inconsistent with the observations that are made to test it, then the concept of 'stuff' that is built into the laws has to be changed.

Phlogiston, which Larmer himself mentions in a slightly different context (66, 68), was one sort of stuff, in this case a negative form of mass, that was postulated in order to retain, in a new form, the principle of the conservation of mass, which was fundamental to the chemistry of that time.

More successful, it still seems, was Einstein's famous formula, $E = mc^2$, which changed the concept of stuff, so that instead of two fundamentally distinct kinds of stuff, mass and energy, there was claimed to be a single kind, mass/energy, with its various different forms. Neither mass nor energy, conceived as distinct, could survive as stuff, since neither was conserved in nuclear reactions. Treated as one kind of stuff, quantitatively related by the formula, conservation is restored. Mass/energy is not directly observable, and so both its nature and its existence can be established only through the scientific laws to which its conservation is fundamental. Consequently, any evidence for a miracle in Larmer's sense, which would involve a change in the total sum of mass/energy, would be just as challenging to the laws of nature involved as any other observational anomaly.

It would seem, then, that whatever form miracles may take, if they override the course of nature in any way, then they do challenge the truth of physicalism and do not merely swallow it up.

It does not follow from this that miracles cannot happen. Rather, it follows that we cannot spell out on a priori grounds, as Larmer tries to do, in what way they can happen. They *may* occur by the creation or annihilation of mass/energy, but they may also occur by a change in the *qualities* of mass/energy, that is, by an exception to the laws of nature. In either case, provided these events are quite rare, we can justify our belief in the existing laws and conditions by accepting that they are universally true and unchanging *except* when God intervenes.

This need not prevent us from enquiring into how these miraculous changes do come about. If, as Larmer suggests (24), human actions also involve an agent causation that runs counter to scientific explanation, then it is nevertheless true that the human agent, so far as we can tell, acts upon the physical world at very specific places in the nervous system. If we are to have a complete understanding of the whole of reality, then we must try to discover just how these actions occur and, similarly, how and under what conditions miracles occur: whether, for example, God does act only by creating or annihilating energy or whether he uses a larger repertoire of miraculous interventionist devices.

I do not wish to claim that such an account, in either case, is likely to be true. I do not myself believe that miracles occur, so I do not need to find out *how* they occur. And I am what is pejoratively called a "soft" determinist, so I am not searching for an undetermined free act.

My reason for engaging briefly in these speculations is rather to give examples of the sort of enquiry in which the person who believes that there are miracles or that there are undetermined free acts needs to engage. There is a tendency amongst some theists to make a virtue of what may be our necessary failure to understand the mysterious ways in which God moves his wonders to perform. But if God did create this universe, which seems to operate for the most part in such a beautifully lawful way, surely we should at least try to use the reason he has given us to find an equally beautiful and complete account of the way in which he miraculously acts upon it.

I must now return to consider apparent exceptions to my claim that a constant quantity of stuff is an essential component of any acceptable system of laws of nature. One of these is the so-called "steady-state hypothesis" of continuous creation put forward some forty years ago by Sir Fred Hoyle of Cambridge University.[2] This theory is an alternative to the "big-bang" theory of the origin of the universe, which is a retrodiction based on the fact that the universe is expanding at a measurable rate. It seems to follow from this fact that at one time the universe occupied a very small space, and must have exploded out from there. Hoyle's theory, if I understand it correctly, is that while the stuff of the universe is indeed moving apart, it did not all start from a single point but has been, and continues to be, gradually created throughout the universe at just the rate that maintains a steady state in the concentration of mass/energy everywhere. On this view it would seem that there is no conservation principle for mass/energy.

One possible answer to this conclusion is to suggest that the lack of a conservation principle for the fundamental stuff of

Hoyle's theory may explain why it has not been widely accepted in the scientific world. There may be, and probably should be, a feeling that this is not a satisfactory explanation, just because it leaves unexplained the changes in the amount of stuff.

It might, perhaps, be argued that the process of continuous creation requires no further explanation: that since it is unchanging in its *rate*, there is a sort of conservation of change that is all that is required. However, I feel that Hoyle's theory, like Larmer's, is one that cries out for completion by an explanation of the process of creation: Why does it take place at just that rate, and how does it happen?

Of course, even the big-bang theory or, indeed, any cosmological theory that calls for a creation of the universe seems to conflict with the first form of the principle of the conservation of mass/energy, as Larmer claims: "Once we accept the claim that energy can neither be created nor destroyed, it makes no sense to talk of God creating the universe, since the universe, being composed of different forms of energy, must be conceived as *uncreated* and indestructible" (25–6).

However, I am not convinced that they really do conflict. On the one hand, since God is held to be eternal, outside time, the concept of His acting is at best fuzzy. So it may be no more fuzzy to regard His act of creation as something that is itself outside time and that therefore does not entail that there was a time *before* the act of creation at which there was no universe in existence. That is, the universe thus created could be of infinite duration in both the past and the future.

If this is really as incomprehensible as it seems to me, one might, on the other hand, point out that the creation of the *whole* universe involves not only the creation of mass/energy but also the implicit creation of the concepts of time and space, since it is meaningless to talk of time or space if there are no temporal events or spatial entities. Consequently, the creation of the universe does not violate *any* conservation principle, since such a principle can only be meaningfully asserted of a period of time; that is, a period during which such things do exist.

These two alternatives may in fact be the same, since the denial that the creation of the universe is an event in time (rather like the denial that a person's own death is an event in his or her life),[3] entails that God does not Himself exist before the creation in any non-eternal sense, since if He did, time would also exist before the creation.

In conclusion, I must stress that I am not arguing either that miracles occur or that they do not occur but only that Larmer's account of the miraculous creation and annihilation of stuff is just as challenging to existing scientific theory as an account involving temporary changes in the properties of that same stuff. In either case, provided the miraculous events remain relatively infrequent, they can be seen as occasional abnormalities that do not require any modification of specific scientific laws but rather a recognition that these laws do not apply with absolute universality. It is true that Larmer's account leaves the actual nature of things inviolate, while even the temporary suspension of the laws of nature themselves implies a change in the very essence of ultimate reality; yet there seems to be no reason to suppose that an omnipotent God would choose to act in the former way rather than the latter, and certainly no reason to suppose that He (or She or It) would have to do so of necessity.

Nonetheless, Larmer's theory is a useful contribution to the debate, since, as I have suggested, though the occurrence of miracles would in the end leave much scientific theory unchanged once the events were recognised as genuinely miraculous, it would still be necessary to explain how such events take place. The lack of regularity that is held to characterise agent causation might make such an explanation difficult to discover, but at least it might be possible to establish just what kind or kinds of interventions in the regularities of nature are involved. The theory that Larmer advocates remains one of the alternative possibilities, but one that would have to be established, if it is to be established at all, by empirical investigation rather than philosophical argument.[4]

NOTES

1 Robert A.H. Larmer, *Water into Wine?* (Kingston and Montreal: McGill-Queen's University Press 1988), chapter 2 and passim. All parenthetical page references in the text are to this book; see also this volume, chap. 3.

2 See "Steady-state hypothesis" in A. Bullock and O. Stallybrass, eds., *The Harper Dictionary of Modern Thought* (New York: Harper & Row 1977), 600.

3 Ludwig Wittgenstein, *Tractatus Logico-Philosophicus*, section 6.4311.
4 In writing this article, I have benefited from helpful discussions with Dr. Larmer of earlier versions of it, including the commentary that he presented at the Annual Congress of the Canadian Philosophical Association in May 1989.

7 Miracles and Conservation Laws: A Reply to MacGill

ROBERT LARMER

My purpose in this chapter is to reply to Professor MacGill's criticisms of my views on miracles (this volume, chap. 6). I shall begin by discussing what I take to be his central objection and then move on to consider his subsidiary objections.

He is quite right to point out that my argument that a miracle need not be conceived as violating any of the laws of nature depends upon drawing a distinction between the laws of nature and the stuff of nature, the behaviour of which the laws describe. As I argued in chapter 3 of this book, we do not violate the laws of motion if we toss an extra ball into a group of balls in motion on a billiard table, but we do produce an outcome that would not otherwise occur. Similarly, God, by producing more of the stuff to which the laws of nature apply, may produce an event that would not otherwise occur, without violating or suspending any of the laws of nature. God might, for example, produce the miracle of the loaves and fishes by creating loaves and fishes *ex nihilo*. He would not thereby violate any of the laws of nature that apply to the behaviour of the matter making up the loaves and fishes. The laws would still apply, there would just be more stuff for them to apply to. In *Water Into Wine?* I go on to show how this account can be generalized to cover all miracles.

It will not do to reply that my account implies the violation of at least one law of nature, namely, the principle of the conservation of energy, because, as I also argued in chapter 3, above, we can distinguish between two forms of the principle: a strong form, which states that energy can neither be created nor destroyed, and a weak form, which states only that energy is conserved in an isolated system. All that is required by the scientific data is the second form of the principle, which in no way precludes the creation or annihilation of energy. The view that we could conceivably produce further evidence establishing the strong form as the correct deep structural assumption that explains the truth of the weak form is entirely mistaken; there is not, indeed, cannot be such a body of evidence. Indeed, as MacGill notes, my view is that miracles disconfirm the strong form of the principle, since they demonstrate that energy can be created and thus that some other deep structural explanation of the truth of the weak form of the principle must be sought.

His basic objection to my account is that conservation laws play a far more fundamental role in scientific explanation than I allow. He argues that "the stuff [to which the laws apply] consists in theoretical entities ... which can be understood only in virtue of their role in the scientific laws in which their names and descriptions occur. And an essential feature in the testing and hence the truth of such laws is that the stuff to which they refer must remain constant in quantity ... [Thus] any evidence for a miracle ... which would involve a change in the total sum of mass/energy would be just as challenging to the laws of nature involved as any other observational anomaly."

I do not think that this claim is correct. If it were, we would expect that if the universe contained either more or less energy than it actually does, then the laws of nature would be other than they actually are. This implies that it would be impossible for scientists to say what a universe with either more or less mass would be like, since its laws would be different and scientists would have no basis for prediction.

Scientists, however, typically assume that a universe that has, say, n units of mass/energy will exhibit the same laws of nature as a universe that contains some other amount of mass/energy, say m units. A good example is the hotly debated question of whether the universe will eventually collapse in upon itself or continue to expand forever. Astronomers will tell you that the answer to this question depends on how dense the universe is, that is, on how much mass/energy it contains, and research is going on to try to determine just how much mass/energy there is. Two assumptions governing this investigation, however, are that the amount of mass/energy in the universe cannot be deduced from the laws of nature and that, whether the universe contains n units of mass/energy or some other amount, the laws of nature remain the same. It seems difficult, therefore, to reconcile MacGill's claim with actual scientific practice. True, the actual history of the universe will be different depending on the amount of mass/energy it contains, but this is a consequence not of the fact that the laws of nature would be different if it contained a different amount of mass/energy but of the fact that there would be a different amount of the stuff whose behaviour the laws describe.

Indeed, MacGill seems to realize that his claim is problematic. He considers as a possible disconfirmation of his view Hoyle's "steady state" hypothesis of continuous creation, but remarks that Hoyle's theory has been generally abandoned. He is correct in saying this but wrong in suggesting that it was abandoned on the grounds that it violated conservation laws. It was abandoned not because it violated conservation laws, though scientists were not entirely comfortable with the idea of continuous creation, but because the empirical evidence needed to confirm the theory was not forthcoming.[1] If MacGill were correct in his claim that it is conceptual nonsense to suppose that the laws of nature might remain the same even if the amount of mass/energy in the universe varies, then scientists should have felt no need to take Hoyle's theory seriously, much less subject it to empirical testing.

Nor is Hoyle's theory the only exception to MacGill's claim. As he notes himself, any theory that implies either the creation or beginning of the universe seems to conflict with the strong form of the principle of the conservation of energy, the claim that energy can neither be created nor destroyed. Any theological claim that God created the universe appears to be ruled out a priori, since the universe, being composed of different forms of energy, would have to be conceived as *uncreated* or indestructible. Likewise, the generally accepted scientific theory of the "big-bang" appears to be ruled out, since it implies that the mass/energy making up the universe had a beginning and thus that the strong form of the principle is false.

MacGill attempts to get around this difficulty by raising certain puzzles concerning the notion of time. He first raises the possibility that God's act of creation might be conceived as taking place outside time and therefore, even if the universe is created, there need not be a time before the act of creation at which there was no universe in existence. Thus, a created universe could be of infinite duration in both the past and future.

He finds this possibility incomprehensible, however, and suggests that the difficulty can be better resolved by realizing "that the creation of the *whole* universe involves not only the creation of mass/energy but also the implicit creation of the concepts of time and space, since it is meaningless to talk of time or space if there are no temporal events or spatial entities. Consequently, the creation of the universe does not violate *any* conservation principle, since such a principle can only be meaningfully asserted of a period of time during which such things do exist."

His first suggestion is one that was made long ago by Aquinas, namely, that the contingency of the universe does not depend on its having a beginning in time. I do not find the notion of God acting outside time so incomprehensible as MacGill, but I fail to see how appealing to it could resolve his difficulty. What he fails to realize is that the strong form of the principle implies not only that the universe had no beginning but also that it had no cause. It does, therefore, rule out a priori the possibility that God created, that is, caused, the universe and hence that theism is true.

Neither does MacGill's second suggestion help. He wants to say that since the absolute beginning of the universe cannot be considered an event in time, the fact that the universe had a beginning does not imply the falsity of the strong form of the principle. This is a mistake. Whether the beginning of the universe was an event in time or time began, so to speak, with the beginning of the universe is irrelevant, since the strong form of the principle implies that the universe could have no beginning whatever. To claim that energy can neither be created nor destroyed is to claim that energy can neither begin to exist nor cease to exist, and this will remain true whether we conceive of the absolute beginning of energy as an event in time or an event that is not in time. The strong form of the principle of the conservation of energy implies, therefore, the falsity not only of theological accounts of the universe but also of the scientifically accepted "Big-Bang" theory.

MacGill's central claim is, therefore, false. It cannot be established on conceptual grounds, it rules out a priori any possibility that theism could be true, and it runs counter both to the well-established big-bang theory and to the fact that scientists routinely assume that the laws of nature would be the same whether the universe contains n units of mass/energy or some other amount. It is simply not the case that a necessary condition of the laws of nature being true is that energy can neither be created nor destroyed.

This does not mean that I disagree with MacGill's claim that the creation of the universe is consistent with the truth of the principle of the conservation of energy if that principle is properly understood and formulated. But I do disagree that one can accept the strong form of the principle and yet make this claim. The only form of the principle that permits this claim to be true, indeed, the only form of the principle that is scientific is the weak form, the claim that energy is conserved in an isolated system. However, it follows from accepting this weak form of the principle that God can create or annihilate energy without violating any of the laws of nature. MacGill is wrong, therefore, to claim that my account of the miraculous creation and annihilation of stuff is just as challenging to existing scientific theory as the traditional violation model of miracles. My account does not challenge any genuine scientific law but rather the gratuitous metaphysical assumption that energy can neither be created nor destroyed.

I pass now to his other objections to my position. One of these, which I think is just, is that I do not make it entirely clear whether miracles do not violate the laws of nature or only that they need not. To clarify my position: it is my view that miracles do not violate the laws of nature, because I think that physical events, including miracles, can be described in terms of a certain amount and ordering of mass/energy and that if an event can be conceived in this way, then so can a particular amount and ordering of mass/energy. If this is true, then for any miracle, it would always be possible for a transcendent agent to produce it by the creation or annihilation of mass/energy, since all that is required is that the agent bring about the particular amount and ordering of mass/energy for the miracle.[2] Given that my account contains advantages over the "violation-model," and given that it can be generalized to cover any conceivable miracle, I see no reason to think miracles ever violate the laws of nature.

It is true that I do not try to prove that miracles cannot violate the laws of nature, but I do not see how it follows from this that my discussion of the evidence required to establish the occurrence of a miracle is flawed. MacGill seems to think that I must make explicit reference to the creation or annihilation of mass/energy, but this is incorrect. If my account of miracles is the correct one, as I have just argued, and if there is good evidence that a miracle has occurred, then there is also good evidence that mass/energy has been created or annihilated. Perhaps, however, he and I will not disagree on this point now that I have made clear that my view is not simply that miracles need not violate the laws of nature but that they do not.

His final objection is that there is a tendency on the part of theists to make a virtue out of the mysterious ways in which God acts. He suggests that "if we are to have a complete understanding of the whole of reality, then we must try to discover how and under what conditions miracles occur." This is imperative for the theist, since "if God did create this universe, which seems to operate in such a beautifully lawful way, surely we should at least try to use the reason he has given us to find an equally beautiful ... account of the way ... he miraculously acts upon it."

I can hardly disagree with him if he means simply to assert that we should try to understand reality as completely as possible. Where I suspect we will part company is over the form legitimate explanations may take. MacGill, as a soft determinist, will be inclined to opt for an explanation in terms of laws and will probably attempt to find the necessary and sufficient physical conditions that will guarantee the occurrence of a miracle. I, on the other hand, think that explanations in terms of agent causality are not only legitimate but more fundamental than explanations in terms of law and that the conditions under which a miracle can be expected to occur relate not so much to the physical as to the moral realm. This, however, seems a convenient stopping place for our discussion. I say this not because I expect that Professor MacGill and I have reached agreement but because, until he becomes persuaded that miracles actually occur, our discussion of the conditions under which they take place is scarcely liable to prove useful.

NOTES

1 See, for example, Ivan R. King, *The Universe Unfolding* (San Francisco: W.H. Freeman 1976), 462.
2 See Robert A. Larmer, *Water Into Wine?* (Montreal: McGill-Queen's University Press 1988), 29.

8 Miracles and Criteria

ROBERT LARMER

Commentators sometimes object that although the concept of miracle may be logically coherent,[1] and although there may be extraordinary occurrences that one might be tempted to call "miracles," one must never actually do so, since this would impose arbitrary limits on what is scientifically explicable. Guy Robinson, in developing this objection, writes:

notice what would happen to the scientist if he allowed himself to employ the concept of an irregularity in nature or of a miracle in relation to his work. He would be finished as a scientist ... To do this would be simply to resign, to opt out, as a scientist ... Scientific development would either be stopped or else made completely capricious, because it would necessarily be a matter of whim whether one invoked the concept of miracle or irregularity to explain an awkward result, or, on the other hand, accepted the result as evidence of the need to modify the theory one was investigating.[2]

In essence, the objection is that because there are no criteria by which to determine whether "anomalies" are properly regarded as miracles or as events that indicate an inadequate understanding of natural processes, it is impossible to justify the use of the term "miracle." Presumably, to invoke the term is to set artificial and arbitrary limits on scientific explanation.

It may be agreed that not every way of postulating a miracle deserves consideration and that a superstitious mentality in which miracles proliferate is to be avoided. It must be questioned, however, whether it is impossible to develop criteria that would distinguish events properly termed miracles from events that are properly understood as indices of inadequate understanding of natural processes.

Suppose, in the case of a particular event, that the following criteria are met:

1 There is strong evidence that the event actually occurred.
2 Although it is carefully scrutinized, the event cannot be identified as being of some repeatable type. (The event need not be absolutely unique but merely not consistently repeatable).
3 The regularity to which the event constitutes an exception is strongly confirmed and is known to apply to the same type of physical circumstances in which the event in question happened.
4 The event is extraordinary, that is to say, it differs greatly from what one would normally expect.
5 The event took place in a moral and religious context and has moral and religious significance.[3]

Surely these criteria would serve to differentiate events that might legitimately be interpreted as miracles from events that would be best interpreted as indices of an inadequate understanding of natural processes. Whether one views an extraordinary event as a miracle or as a result of some unknown or poorly understood natural processes need not be a matter of whim.

A possible objection to this line of argument is that although it may not be a matter of caprice or whim whether one terms an event a miracle, miracle claims, no less than scientific claims, are corrigible. To term an event a miracle, however, is to hold that the event is explained and to rule out the possibility of any future scientific explanation.

Such an objection fails. Two of the criteria for an event to be considered a miracle are that it cannot be identified as an event of some repeatable type and that the regularity of nature to which it constitutes an exception is strongly confirmed and known to apply to the type of physical circumstances in which the event happened. Clearly, however, there could be new scientific evidence suggesting either that the event can be identified as being of some repeatable type or that the regularity of nature to which the event constitutes an exception is not as strongly established as once was thought. In terming an event a miracle, one does not, therefore, prematurely rule out the possibility of a future scientific explanation of the event.

There is another, related objection based on the fact that miracle claims are corrigible, which maintains that it is always more rational to believe that an event could be explained naturalistically, if only we had the requisite scientific knowledge, than to believe that a miracle has occurred. In assessing the force of this objection, one must distinguish between pragmatic working assumptions and metaphysical presuppositions. One may endorse the principle of first seeking a naturalistic explanation of an event without thereby being committed to the position that a supernatural explanation can never be legitimately postulated. Geisler is correct when he writes: "Simply to assume ... that there must be a naturalistic explanation for every event begs the question in favour of naturalism ... adopting the working procedure of always looking for a natural explanation need not be extended into a rigid naturalistic position that there are no non-natural explanations. The scientific mind should not legislate what kind of explanations there can be.[4]

There is, of course, always the logical possibility that a revision of scientific law may lead to a naturalistic explanation of what was hitherto considered a miracle. This fact, however, does not in itself justify the claim that it is always more rational to believe that all events have naturalistic explanations. The fact that a claim is corrigible does not entail the conclusion that other logically possible claims are more probably true.

For example, since all scientific claims are corrigible, it is always logically possible that we are wrong in supposing that, in the normal course of events, the blood circulates in a living human body. It will hardly do, however, merely on the grounds that this claim is corrigible, to claim that some other logically possible alternative, such as the claim that we are mistaken in believing the blood to circulate, is equally probable or as well-established.

It is logically possible that some revision of scientific law might permit a naturalistic explanation of events one is tempted to term miraculous, but it is also logically possible that no revision would enable one to offer a naturalistic explanation. One's decision concerning which of these alternatives is most probably true must be based on an assessment of evidence. Both alternatives may be logically possible, but they are not necessarily equally probable.

Let us consider an example. Suppose one hears of a man who claims to perform miracles of healing through the power of God. Upon investigating, one learns that this person has not only an exemplary character but also an apparent ability to perform remarkable cures. One is able to capture on film occasions when, immediately following the prayers of this man, fingers lost to leprosy were regrown to their original form and length in a matter of seconds, and occasions when eyes severely burned by acid were immediately restored to sight. One finds, further, not only that this man appears to have the power to heal any kind of disease or injury but also that no interposition of lead screens or strong electromagnetic fields or the like has any effect on his apparent ability to heal. Indeed, it is observed that his power is apparently independent of distance, since people in distant countries have experienced dramatic healing after this man prayed for their cure.

Such an example raises at least two major problems for the person who holds that it is always more reasonable to postulate a natural cause rather than the occurrence of a miracle.

The first is that such a procedure commits one to an apparently unwarranted scepticism concerning our knowledge of natural law. If one has good reason to accept the fact that such extraordinary events have occurred and if one insists that all explanations of physical events must be naturalistic, then one must be prepared to reject or revise the laws that led one to expect different results. This places one in the position of questioning what were hitherto thought to be basic, well-evidenced, and accurate statements of natural law. In short, one is forced to adopt a position of radical scepticism concerning the claims of science. This, it should be noted, is in sharp contrast to the position of the defender of the concept of miracle, who is able to offer an account of how one may accept the occurrence of such extraordinary events and yet retain one's faith in what seem to be well-evidenced statements of natural law.

This is neither to deny that revolutions occur in scientific theory nor to deny that science often progresses by rejecting previously accepted statements of natural law. However, to insist on a naturalistic interpretation of such phenomena as have been described merely on the basis of general remarks about falsifiability and revolution in science is at least as great an act of faith as any religious interpretation of such events.

Indeed, it may require a greater act of faith to interpret such events naturalistically. The defender of the concept of miracle, taking his cue from Hume, may ask in a particular instance which is more likely: that a multitude of unknown processes requiring us to radically revise or even reject well-established statements of natural law have fortuitously combined to produce an extraordinary and religiously significant event; or that an extraordinary and religiously significant event has occurred that, although it does not force us to revise or reject any well-established statements of natural law, does seem to indicate a transcendent rational agent has acted to produce in nature an event that nature could not, of itself, produce.[5] Surely only a somewhat dogmatic and uncritical metaphysical assumption that nature is in fact an isolated system can explain the insistence of some thinkers that, no matter what the event and no matter what the context in which it occurs, it is always more rational to live in the faith that such an event has a naturalistic explanation than to believe it to be a miracle.

The second major objection that the defender of naturalistic interpretation, no matter what the event or its context, must meet is that the very nature of the extraordinary powers of a "miracle" worker might conceivably preclude a naturalistic explanation of these powers.

One wonders, for example, what it could mean to term the power to heal a "natural" power if it was shown that the capacity to heal was not affected by distance, by any kind of physical screening, or by the specific disease or injury of the person in need of healing. Could one legitimately use the word "natural" to describe a capacity that appears to be independent of other natural forces and capacities? To insist that it is legitimate to describe such a capacity as natural is to open oneself to the charge that one has rendered one's position invulnerable by making it untestable and hence unfalsifiable. One cannot hold that naturalistic explanation is compatible with any logically possible state of affairs in the physical world without leaving oneself vulnerable to such a charge.

The defender of naturalistic interpretation may, of course, note that it would be difficult to show that a certain ability is truly independent of physical limitations. There is always the logical possibility that new evidence will show that it is not. This defense is certainly true, but it leaves the defender of naturalistic interpretation in the awkward position of justifying his rejection of evidence to the contrary. Evidence for a particular scientific claim is never conclusive or, indeed, complete; one must always reach provisional conclusions on the basis of the evidence available. Provisional conclusions may be strongly established, however, and, in the absence of evidence suggesting different conclusions, they deserve rational assent. As in the example just developed, there could conceivably bet instances where an abundance of evidence seems to indicate the exercise of capacities that are independent of physical limitations.

One cannot hold that one must always postulate a naturalistic explanation of an event, however improbable that explanation may be, unless one also holds that it has been firmly established beyond possible dispute that nature is an isolated system suffering no intrusions from something other than itself. Unless one is prepared to make the latter assertion a priori, it is difficult to make the former statement without begging the question of miracle.

NOTES

1 I define a miracle as an extraordinary and religiously significant physical event that never would have occurred except through the relatively immediate action of a rational agent who, in some way, transcends nature.

2 Guy Robinson, "*Miracles*," *Ratio*, 9, no. 2 (1967): 155–66.

3 Phrases like "moral and religious significance" tend to be somewhat vague. The point I am trying to make in introducing this criterion is made very well by Ramm: "It may be safely asserted that a hypoth-

esis does not receive fair treatment if viewed disconnected from its
system, and further, that any hypothesis proposed must make peace
with the system that it is associated with – even to revolutionising
the system, e.g., Copernicus and Einstein. It is therefore impossible
to see miracles in the Christian perspective if viewed only as problems of science and history, i.e., to use only historical and scientific
categories for interpretation. It is not asked that miracles be accepted blindly simply because they are associated with the Christian system; nor do we argue in a circle asking one to view miracles
from the Christian position to see them as true when the Christian
system is the point at issue. No hypothesis in science is confirmed
until tentatively accepted as true. The tentative acceptation does
not prove the hypothesis but it is absolutely necessary to test the
hypothesis." (Bernard Ramm, *Protestant Christian Evidences*(Chicago,
Moody Press 1953), 129.
4 Norman Geisler, *Christian Apologetics* (Grand Rapids, MI: Baker Books
1976), 272.
5 Cf. David Hume's "Of Miracles," in *Enquiries Concerning the Human
Understanding and Concerning the Principles of Morals*, ed. L.A. Selby-
Bigge, 2d ed. (1902; Oxford: Oxford University Press 1972),
109–31. Note especially the paragraph beginning, "The plain consequence ..." (115).

9 Miracles and Naturalistic Explanations

DAVID BASINGER

In chapter 8, Robert Larmer attacks the contention that "it is always more rational to believe that an event could be explained naturalistically, if only we had the requisite scientific knowledge, than to believe that a miracle has occurred." It is perfectly justifiable, he acknowledges, to seek initially for a naturalistic explanation for a physical event. And it is logically possible that some revision of scientific law might enable us some day to offer a naturalistic explanation for any given event that cannot presently be explained naturalistically. But it is also logically possible, he continues, that no revision would enable us to offer a naturalistic explanation for some such events. Accordingly, "one's decision concerning which of these alternatives is most probably true must be based on an assessment of evidence." And there are conceivable situations, he argues, in which the evidence would not make it most reasonable to hold out for a natural explanation. He offers the example of a man "who has not only an exemplary character but also an apparent ability to heal any kind of disease or injury ... no interposition of lead screens or ... the like has any effect on his apparent ability to heal ... Indeed ... his power is apparently independent of distance."

Why would it be so hard in this case "to postulate a natural cause rather than the occurrence of a miracle"? For one thing, Larmer tells us, it would force us to adopt a position of radical scepticism concerning the claims of science. "If one has good reason to accept the fact that such extraordinary events have occurred and if one insists that all explanation of physical events must be natural, then one must be prepared to reject the laws that led one to expect different results." But the defender of miracles, we are told, does not have this problem. He or she can acknowledge the occurrence of the event and "yet retain [his or her] faith in what seem to be basic, well-evidenced, and accurate statements of natural law." Accordingly, he continues, it is difficult to see how a religious interpretation could be considered any less reasonable in this case. And this fact in turn leads Larmer to conclude that "surely only a somewhat dogmatic and uncritical metaphysical assumption that nature is in fact an isolated system can explain the insistence of some thinkers that, no matter what the event and no matter what the context in which it occurs, it is always more rational to live in the faith that such an event has a natural explanation rather than believe it to be a miracle."

Larmer's argument, it seems to me, contains two basic confusions. First, is it true that if someone grants the occurrence of the type of extraordinary event Larmer cites and yet still wants to hold out for natural causation, she "must be prepared to reject or revise the laws that led [her] to expect different results"? I think not.

It is true that scientists must assume the working hypothesis that current natural laws express what will always happen under certain conditions. And it is also the case that any counterinstance to a current law necessitates a reevaluation of the "law" in question. But as philosophers like Richard Swinburne have repeatedly pointed out, natural laws are not merely summary statements of what does in fact happen. Nor do they describe in some a priori fashion what in fact can or cannot happen. Natural laws, rather, describe events only in so far as they take place in a *predictable and regular manner.*[2] Accordingly, there is no reason to grant that when faced with a seeming counterinstance, we are under some mandate either to admit that the event occurred as reported and abandon the relevant law or to affirm the relevant law and deny that the event actually occurred. If a seeming counterinstance proves to be *repeatable*, then the current laws in question certainly must be abandoned (or modified). But otherwise, we can, in principle, affirm both the counterinstance and the law in question.

To do so will not, as Larmer implies, render the laws in question nonfunctional or turn science into a quasi-metaphysical guessing game. For as long as the recalcitrant event is not repeatable, it furnishes us with no basis upon which to build an alternative to the current natural laws in question. Such laws can remain (indeed must remain) the working hypotheses that the scientist utilizes.

But what of Larmer's more important claim that to hold that it is always most rational to deny supernatural causal intervention is a dogmatic, uncritical, question-begging assumption. He makes this claim, remember, because he believes that there are conceivable situations in which the "evidence" makes belief in supernatural causation most reasonable. But is this so? Are there such conceivable cases?

There may well be situations that, *when considered in isolation*, make divine interventions a very plausible causal hypothesis. But when assessing a causal hypothesis, one must consider all the relevant data. Applied to Larmer's example, this means that we must not only determine, as Larmer implies, whether divine causation is the most plausible explanation for the "healing" alone; we must also determine whether the existence of an interventive God is compatible with all other experiential data. We must, for example, consider whether the existence of an interventive God is compatible with all the evil we experience.

Now let us assume that in comparing the plausibility of affirming that God has healed the individuals in question (and, thus, that God's existence is compatible with the amount and types of evil in the world) with the plausibility of affirming that God's existence is not compatible with such evils (and, thus, that God did not heal the individuals in question) someone decides that God's nonexistence is more plausible overall. In other words, let us assume that the prima facie evidence for God's existence that has been generated by the healing is not of sufficient weight in the mind of a given individual to make the theistic perspective the most plausible overall. Could Larmer justifiably accuse such an individual of assuming an uncritical, dogmatic, question-begging stance?

I believe not. To substantiate such a charge, he would need

to stipulate some set of objective criteria initially accepted by both the theist and nontheist in relation to which it could be shown that, given the healings in question, nontheism could no longer be considered an acceptable worldview for any rational person. But to what mutually acceptable set of criteria could he appeal? What set of criteria would allow him to demonstrate objectively that the evidence for God's existence generated by the remarkable healings must be seen by all rational people as outweighing, for example, the seeming evidence against God's existence generated by the amount and types of evil we experience?

I am not convinced that such criteria exist. Both theists and nontheists normally agree that the affirmation of an inconsistent set of beliefs is irrational. But there is no agreement on criteria for "weighting" various experimental perspectives. Some nontheists contend that the evidence against God's existence, evil, for example, is such that no amount of conceivable additional evidence for God's existence could ever counterbalance it. Other nontheists are more tentative at this point. Some theists contend that their personal experience with God is so self-authenticating that no amount of conceivable evidence against God's existence could outweigh it. Other theists are more cautious in their assessment of the situation. Each is willing to consider the evidence; each considers his or her perspective to be most rational. I, personally, can think of no objective, non-question-begging basis for resolving this metaphysical stalemate. I must agree with Alvin Plantinga that the probability with respect to belief or disbelief in God (which is necessary for belief in divine causation) is ultimately relative to one's own noetic structure.[2]

Accordingly, it seems to me that there is little basis upon which to claim that all proponents of solely natural causation build on dogmatic, uncritical, question-begging reasoning. To claim emphatically that there is *in fact* no God (and thus no divine causal intervention) may be an unwarranted metaphysical contention. But the nontheist need not be making any such ontological claim. She can simply be saying that while this epistemological contention is debatable, its affirmation is not necessarily any more dogmatic or question-begging than the belief that the "total" evidence makes theistic belief (and thus the possibility of divine intervention) most reasonable.

NOTES

1 Richard Swinburne, *The Concept of Miracle* (London: Macmillan 1970), 29–32.
2 Alvin Plantinga, "The Probabilistic Argument from Evil," *Philosophical Studies* 35 (1979): 1–53.

10 Miracles and Naturalistic Explanations: A Rejoinder

ROBERT LARMER

In the last chapter, David Basinger takes issue with a claim I advanced in chapter 8, where I attacked the view that it is always more rational to believe that an event could be explained naturalistically, if only we had the requisite scientific knowledge, than to believe that a miracle has occurred. In its place I advanced the counterclaim that only a dogmatic and uncritical assumption that nature is in fact an isolated system can explain the insistence of some thinkers that, no matter what the event and no matter what the context in which it occurs, it is always more rational to live in the faith that the event has a naturalistic explanation than to believe it a miracle. Basinger thinks that my argument contains two basic confusions, but I think both his objections are mistaken and, consequently, that his attempted refutation fails.

His first criticism concerns my claim that there are conceivable situations in which the evidence would not make it more reasonable to hold out for a naturalistic explanation of certain events than to postulate supernatural intervention. On the basis of a thought experiment concerning a healer of exemplary character who claims to perform miracles of healing and whose remarkable ability to cure any type of disease or injury is apparently unaffected by physical circumstances, I argued that if one had good reason to believe that such events had occurred and in such a context, and if one insisted that all explanations of physical events must be natural, then one would have to be prepared to reject or revise the laws that led one to expect different results. This, I argued, would force one to adopt a position of radical scepticism concerning the claims of science, since it would force one to question what were hitherto thought to be basic, well-evidenced, and accurate statements of natural law. I further argued that the theist can avoid this dilemma, since he can offer an account of how one may accept the occurrence of such extraordinary events, yet retain faith in what seem to be accurate statements of the laws of nature.[1]

In response, Basinger argues that I have misunderstood what natural laws are. Following Richard Swinburne, he argues that the laws of nature are not merely summary statements of what does in fact happen, and that they do not describe in some a priori fashion what must happen, but rather that they describe events only insofar as they take place in a predictable and regular manner. He takes this to show that the naturalist is not faced with the dilemma of either admitting the occurrence of a highly unusual event and revising or abandoning the relevant law or affirming the relevant law and denying that the event occurred. So long as a counterinstance, that is, an unusual event, is non-repeatable, the naturalist may affirm both the occurrence of the event and the validity of the relevant law, since the law is conceived only as describing events that are repeatable.

I agree that natural laws are not merely summary statements of what does in fact happen. I also agree that they do not describe what must happen. I have some reservations about Basinger's statement that natural laws describe events that take place in a predictable and regular manner, since laws by themselves do not allow prediction of specific events, but rather laws in conjunction with a set of initial conditions. Nothing of importance for the present discussion hangs on this last claim, however, since my objections can be formulated independently of it.

Where I disagree is with his claim that granting all this enables the naturalist to escape my proposed dilemma. First, calling an event a nonrepeatable counterinstance does not really explain its occurrence. The naturalist, in labelling it in this way, would not be offering an alternative explanation of the event but simply refusing to accept the theist's explanation. This does not seem a rational course of action unless he is prepared to specify why the theist's explanation is mistaken. At the very least, he should be prepared to say why the criteria I proposed for identifying miracles cannot be considered reliable.

Second, even assuming we can bypass this difficulty, the strategy of appealing to nonrepeatable counterinstances in this context is precarious. Swinburne originally introduced this idea in order to make sense of how we could speak of a violation of a law of nature yet deny that there exists any reason to revise the law in the face of an exception. Basinger, however, is employing the notion not for Swinburne's original purpose but to try and show how an event could be conceived as having a natural cause yet be an exception to the laws of nature. It needs to be emphasized that his strategy will work only if the event in question is truly nonrepeatable for, as Basinger himself notes, "if a seeming counterinstance proves to be repeatable, then the current laws in question certainly must be abandoned (or modified)." This seems to imply that his discussion of nonrepeatable counterinstances is irrelevant to my argument, since my example explicitly makes reference to repeatable counterinstances; that is, the healer performs remarkable cures on more than one occasion. Put more generally, my point is that reports of miracles frequently indicate not just the occurrence of an unusual event but the repeated occurrence of events of the same type. Jesus, for example, is reported to have raised the dead not just once but several times. Basinger has not, therefore, provided the naturalist with any escape from my dilemma, unless the event in question is absolutely unique.

His second objection is that my claim that there are conceivable situations in which the "evidence" makes belief in supernatural causation more reasonable depends upon viewing these situations in isolation and not taking into account the overall plausibility of theism. He asks us to consider a case where the prima facie evidence for God's existence that has been generated by a remarkable healing is not of sufficient weight in the mind of an individual to make the theistic perspective more plausible overall and poses the question of whether I could "justifiably accuse such an individual of assuming an uncritical, dogmatic, question-begging stance." He suggests that I could not, unless I could specify in advance some set of objective criteria "in relation to which it could be shown that, given the 'healings' in question, nontheism could no longer be considered an acceptable worldview for any rational person," and he goes on to argue that such criteria do not exist.

I agree with his insistence that the overall plausibility of theism must be taken into account, but I do not think that I have ignored this issue to the degree he suggests, nor do I think that the procedure of assessing plausibility is quite so mechanical as he seems to assume. In reply to his objection, I want to make two points. The first is that if, as he admits, the occurrence of certain remarkable events would provide strong prima facie evidence for theism, then the burden of proof is on the naturalist to show why, if such events occur, the evidence should be rejected or reinterpreted. The only reason that would justify such treatment would be some stronger body of contrary evidence tending to disconfirm theism. Until the naturalist has specified just what this body of evidence is and why it should be interpreted as contrary to the truth of theism, the refusal to admit that supernatural causation of certain remarkable events would be the more rational explanation of their occurrence is uncritical, dogmatic, and question-begging.

Nor is it easy to see what this body of evidence could be. The primary candidate and the one at which Basinger broadly hints is the existence of evil. I do not want to downplay the problem of evil or suggest that its relation to the occurrence of miracles is not an important issue, but I wonder whether Basinger is being consistent in objecting to my position on this basis. The thrust of his article is to suggest that a single occurrence or set of occurrences, for example, dramatic and unusual healings performed in a religiously significant context, is largely irrelevant to the plausibility of theism. But remarks like this cut both ways. Evils, no less than miracles constitute a set of occurrences and if one is prepared to dismiss miracles as largely irrelevant to the plausibility of theism, should one not also regard the existence of evil as irrelevant?

The second point I would like to make is that in chapter 8 I specified a set of objective criteria that would serve to distinguish events properly viewed as miracles from events properly viewed as anomalies. I find it puzzling that even though my chapter was entitled "Miracles and Criteria," Basinger finds it possible to ignore my criteria entirely. Also, although I think the attempt to specify criteria is worthwhile, I wonder if criteria are quite so essential as he suggests. The demand for a set of clearly articulated criteria tends to assume that in the absence of criteria for borderline cases it is impossible to have knowledge of clear cases. But is this really true? There may be cases where we are unsure whether a particular event should be called miraculous, for example, when a believer's house is spared in the midst of a tornado that levels the rest of a suburb, but do we really need to elaborate a set of criteria to recognize a paradigm case, such as the raising of Lazarus, as miraculous?

Finally, even if there is no general agreement between theists and naturalists on weighing the general plausibility of theism, I do not think that this necessarily precludes the possibility of establishing the superiority of one worldview over the other. It has happened in the history of science that two theories have competed without any generally agreed upon criteria for assessing them, but nevertheless one has eventually emerged as clearly superior. If this is possible and rational in the domain of large-scale scientific theories, I see no reason to deny that it is possible in the domain of large-scale philosophical theories.

NOTES

1 This is worked out in detail in my *Water into Wine?* (Montreal: McGill-Queen's University Press 1988).

11 Miracles as Evidence for Theism

DAVID BASINGER

In our ongoing dialogue in this volume, Robert Larmer and I have been discussing whether the undisputed occurrence of certain conceivable events would require all honest, thoughtful individuals to acknowledge that God has supernaturally intervened in earthly affairs. The test case in question is that of a healer of exemplary character with a remarkable ability to cure any type of disease or injury. As Larmer sees it, to hold out for a totally naturalistic explanation in this case would be uncritical, dogmatic, and question-begging. The most rational response would be to acknowledge God's interventive activity.

I initially pointed out in response that when discussing the question of God's existence (which any discussion of divine causal activity obviously presupposes), no single occurrence or set of similar occurrences can justifiably be considered in isolation. Specifically, I pointed out that anyone who believed the healings in question offered prima facie evidence for theism (the belief in the existence of a God who can benevolently intervene in earthly affairs) would also have to consider occurrences that might stand as prima facie evidence against theism – for example, the amount and nature of human pain and suffering we experience – before a final decision was made. And I then went on to argue that if someone acknowledged that these healings, *when considered in isolation*, did appear to be strong evidence for theism but maintained that such evidence did not outweigh what she viewed as the stronger evidence against theism generated by evil, I did not see how her decision could justifiably be considered dogmatic, uncritical, or question-begging.

Larmer, however, is not convinced. It is his belief that if a nontheist acknowledges that certain occurrences stand as strong evidence for theism, then "the burden of proof is on [this person] to show why ... the evidence should be rejected or reinterpreted." Specifically, the nontheist must identify "some stronger body of contrary evidence" and explain "why it should be interpreted as contrary to the truth of theism." If this cannot be done, Larmer concludes, then this individual can still rightly be accused of maintaining "an uncritical, dogmatic, question-begging stance."

Furthermore, Larmer does not find "it easy to see what this body of evidence could be." Specifically, he wonders whether I am "being consistent" when I claim that evil might stand as strong counterevidence in the mind of a nontheist. For if specific occurrences – for example, healings – cannot establish the plausibility of theism, he asks, then how can specific events – for example, instances of evil – establish the implausibility of theism? And thus he stands by his original contention.

It seems to me, though, that Larmer is continuing to confuse two related, but distinct contentions about the relationship between evil and the rejection of theism:

1 The undisputed occurrence of certain instances of evil can (could) justifiably be cited by a person as a compelling basis for the rejection of theism by all knowledgeable, sincere individuals.
2 The undisputed occurrence of certain instances of evil can (could) justifiably be cited by a person as the primary reason why she rejects theism.

If my criticism of Larmer were based on my affirmation of (1) – if I were claiming that the occurrence of certain instances of evil can (could) justifiably be viewed by a nontheist as mandating the rejection of theism by all rational individuals – then I could rightly be accused of wanting it both ways. For I do want to claim that the occurrence of no single event or set of similar events – for instance, certain healings – can (could) justifiably be viewed by a theist as justifiably compelling belief in theism.

But I reject (1). My criticism of Larmer, rather, is based on my affirmation of (2). It is, I am claiming, no less justifiable, in principle, for an individual to consider evil as evidence against theism than it is for an individual to consider healings as evidence for theism. And I am further claiming that just as an individual could acknowledge that evil, *if considered in isolation*, counts as strong evidence against theism and yet justifiably maintain that such disconfirming evidence is outweighed by the evidence she sees as supporting theism – for instance, healings or personal experiences – the reverse is also true. An individual could, in principle, grant that occurrences such as healings, *if considered in isolation*, count as strong evidence for theism and yet justifiably maintain that such evidence is outweighed by the evidence against theism she sees generated by evil.

Now, of course, if it could be demonstrated in some objective, non-question-begging manner either that evil cannot justifiably be viewed as strong evidence against theism or that certain conceivable occurrences supporting theism would necessarily outweigh any counterevidence, then the situation would be different. But neither of these contentions has to my knowledge been established. In fact, I do not see how this could be done. So I believe my criticism of Larmer's position still stands. Healings of the sort he envisions would certainly be startling and would rightly require serious consideration by theists and nontheists alike. Perhaps many nontheists would even come to view such evidence as outweighing the evidence that had previously convinced them to be nontheists, and they would, therefore, "convert." But Larmer has given us no reason to believe that a nontheist who acknowledged certain healings to be strong evidence for theism but did not see such evidence as outweighing what she viewed as the stronger counterevidence, and thus remained a nontheist, could justifiably be accused of being dogmatic and uncritical and of question-begging. In principle, she would not have violated any logical principle nor failed to fulfil any epistemic duty.

12 Miracles, Evidence, and Theism: A Further Apologia

ROBERT LARMER

David Basinger's argument in chapter 11 reveals that we have made some progress in our ongoing discussion of miracles and their relation to the laws of nature and theistic belief. I hope the present chapter will either resolve or further narrow our disagreement.

I do not wish to nitpick, but it is important to note that Basinger's characterization of our discussion is not entirely accurate. He suggests that we "have been discussing whether the undisputed occurrence of certain conceivable events would require all honest, thoughtful individuals to acknowledge that God has supernaturally intervened in earthly affairs." But my original discussion (chapter 8) was intended to refute Guy Robinson's claim that it is always more rational to believe that an event could be explained naturalistically, if only we had the requisite scientific knowledge, than to believe that a miracle has occurred.[1] In response to Robinson, I advanced the counterclaim that only the dogmatic and uncritical assumption that nature is in fact an isolated system can explain the insistence of some thinkers that, no matter what the event and no matter what the context in which it occurs, it is always more rational to live in the faith that it has a naturalistic explanation rather than to believe it a miracle. Nowhere did I explicitly claim that the undisputed oc-currence of certain conceivable events would require all honest, thoughtful individuals to acknowledge that God has supernaturally intervened in earthly affairs. What is true and what did emerge in the course of analyzing the difficulties Robinson faces in trying to make good his argument is that the theist can justifiably defend the claim that Basinger attributes to me. It is not, however, the claim that I explicitly made in my original article, nor is it the claim to which Basinger initially responded.

By way of making clear my original claim, I ask the reader to consider the by now familiar thought-experiment concerning a healer of exemplary character that I described initially in chapter 8. On the basis of this example, I argued that under certain conditions, the naturalist would be forced by the evidence adopt a position of radical scepticism concerning the claims of science, since it would force him to question what were hitherto thought to be basic, well-evidenced, and accurate statements of natural law. I further argued that the theist could avoid this dilemma, since she could offer an account of how one may accept the occurrence of extraordinary events, yet retain faith in what seem to be accurate statements of the laws of nature. This implies that the naturalist would be demonstrating at least as much, and probably more, faith than the theist in holding out for a naturalistic explanation of such events. The naturalist is not entitled, therefore, to claim that it would always be more rational to postulate a naturalistic explanation, no matter what the event or the context in which it occurred.

Basinger's initial criticism (chapter 9) was that my argument was confused on two counts: that I had failed to understand what natural laws are and that I had failed to take into account the overall plausibility of theism when analyzing whether certain conceivable events would best be explained by appealing to supernatural intervention. In reply to his first objection (chapter 10), I pointed out that my understanding of the laws of nature is basically the same as his own. Where we differ, I suggested, is about whether his strategy of labelling an event "a nonrepeatable counterinstance" will enable him to show that it may be an exception to the laws of nature yet have a natural cause. At best, this strategy would work only if the event in question is truly nonrepeatable, that is, absolutely unique, since, as Basinger himself notes (chapter 9), "if a seeming counterinstance proves to be *repeatable*, then the current laws in question certainly must be abandoned (or modified)." The implication is that his discussion of nonrepeatable counterinstances is irrelevant, since my example refers explicitly to repeatable counterinstances, that is, the healer performs remarkable cures on more than one occasion. I argued further that calling an event a nonrepeatable counterinstance does not really explain its occurrence. In labelling it as such and in insisting that it has a natural cause, the naturalist would not be offering an alternative explanation, but simply refusing to accept the theist's explanation. This, I suggested, is not a rational course of action, unless the naturalist is prepared to specify why the theist's explanation is mistaken. At the very least, this would involve him in specifying why the criteria I proposed for identifying miracles cannot be considered reliable.

Since in his response (chapter 11) Basinger makes no reply to these arguments but concentrates instead exclusively on defending his second objection to my position, I will assume that he finds my response to his first objection cogent and will move on to consider his second objection. The crux of this objection is that I failed to take into account the question of the overall plausibility of theism when I suggested that "only a ... dogmatic and uncritical metaphysical assumption that nature is in fact an isolated system can explain the insistence of some thinkers that, no matter what the event and no matter what the context in which it occurs, it is always more rational to live in the faith that such an event has a naturalistic explanation than to believe it to be a miracle" (chapter 8). Basinger admits that "there may well be situations which, *when considered in isolation*, make divine interventions a very plausible causal hypothesis," but insists that the naturalist is not being dogmatic if she judges that this prima facie evidence is not of sufficient weight to overcome her judgment that the amount and type of evil in the world renders belief in God implausible (chapter 9). He goes on to suggest that since there is no "objective, non-question-begging ... [way to demonstrate] that evil cannot justifiably be viewed as strong evidence against theism," it is illegitimate of me to accuse the naturalist of dogmatism.

In reply, two points may be made. First, as I have already mentioned, my original article was an attempt to refute Robinson's claim that it is always more rational to believe an event has a natural explanation than to believe a miracle has occurred. Given that Robinson and those who espouse this position typically make no reference to evil or any other body of evidence taken to disconfirm God's existence, my charge of dogmatism and question-begging on the part of the naturalist is not so far off the mark as Basinger suggests.

Second, even if we allow for the more sophisticated naturalist that Basinger postulates, the argument fails. Basinger makes much of the fact no one has shown that evil cannot justifiably be viewed as strong evidence against theism. He goes on to draw the conclusion that the naturalist can non-dogmatically claim that no matter what are the "miracles" in question and no matter what are the circumstances in which they occur, it is always more rational to believe they have a natural rather than a supernatural explanation. Leaving aside the fact that Basinger's assessment of the problem of evil seems unduly pessimistic, I do not see how his conclusion follows.

How does it follow from the fact that a given body of data permits two equally rational interpretations that these two interpretations will remain equally rational no matter what further data comes to light? More specifically, how does the fact that the theist and the naturalist rationally disagree over whether a certain amount of evil is consistent with the existence of God demonstrate that this disagreement would remain rational no matter what the amount of evil in question or no matter what the number of miracles? The answer, of course, is that it does not. Unless the naturalist is prepared to argue that it is logically impossible that God would allow any evil whatsoever – and I think Basinger will agree that the naturalist will find this position indefensible – she cannot argue that disbelief in God is rational no matter how small in principle the class of evils becomes. Similarly, unless the naturalist is prepared to argue that miracles are logically impossible, she cannot argue that disbelief in miracles is rational no matter what the number, type, or context in which the events in question occur.

Basinger might reply that I have missed the point; that the class of events that might be considered miracles is logically distinct from the class of evils. Since, then, there is agreement on whether or how strongly the amount of evil counts against belief in God, the naturalist is not dogmatic if she holds that this evidence outweighs the evidence generated by events plausibly interpreted as miracles.

This reply would not do. There seems no reason in principle why the positive evidence generated by miracles could not outweigh what the naturalist takes to be the negative evidence generated by evils. Basinger may, perhaps, be correct in suggesting that it is not easy to reach agreement, but this in no way demonstrates that it is not question-begging and dogmatic simply to assume that the body of positive evidence generated by miracles could never, even in principle, persuade all rational persons.

By way of seeing this, let us conduct the following thought experiment. Suppose Basinger's sophisticated naturalist approaches my miracle worker and informs him that, although these "miracles" *considered in isolation*, provide strong evidence for theism, she feels compelled to interpret them naturalistically, since she feels that the disconfirming evidence from the existence of evil is so strong. The miracle worker, rather than analysing the naturalist's faulty philosophical views, asks her to draw up a list of the evils she has in mind and proceeds to work down the list, remedying each evil as he goes. Would there not arrive a point, even before the end of the list is reached, where the naturalist would have to revise her views in favour of theism? Different naturalists might, of course, revise their views at different points, but this in no way demonstrates that there will not be a point at which every rational person will have been convinced.

Such an example seems farfetched, and I am far from wanting to place too much weight on it, but it is no more farfetched than Basinger's claim that the absence of agreement on how rational persons evaluate a certain body of data demonstrates that they could never reach agreement, no matter what the data. Thus, although I agree with Basinger that the overall plausibility of theism must be taken into account, I remain unrepentant in charging the naturalist with dogmatism and question-begging if she insists that we could never, even in principle, be justified in calling an event a miracle.

NOTES

1 Guy Robinson, "Miracles," *Ratio* 9 (1967) 155–66.

13 Authenticating Biblical Reports of Miracles

PHILLIP WIEBE

INTRODUCTION

The historical authenticity of the biblical reports of miracles has often been advanced by experts and lay apologists alike on the ground that the Bible has been shown to be correct on matters that admit of external support, such as the support coming from independent historical documentation and archaeological discoveries. The reports of miraculous incidents have been viewed as gaining substantial credence from the fact that the biblical writers have been found to be accurate in their reports of ordinary historical events. These are not the only grounds, of course, on which the authenticity of such reports has been defended, for apologists have also relied on features of the documents themselves, such as the (near) internal consistency among different documents reporting the same events (for example, healing miracles reported by several synoptic gospel writers), the Semitic character of the writings, the numerous documents that form the basis of the standard text, the alleged absence of mythical elements even in the miracle stories, and so on.[1] But the argument from the accuracy of the reports of what could be called "ordinary events" continues to enjoy popularity, and it is this argument that I wish to examine here. Several examples follow.

F.F. Bruce, in *The New Testament Documents: Are They Reliable?* admits that the chief difficulty in accepting the reliability of the New Testament is the miracle stories found in the gospels. He argues for the authenticity of the New Testament documents, including the reports of miracles, in large part on the ground that the writers have been found to be correct on many small historical matters. Luke is singled out for special attention in this regard. Bruce asserts that "Luke's record entitles him to be regarded as a writer of habitual accuracy."[2] The context of this remark clearly shows that Bruce intends it to be an endorsement of Luke's accuracy in the reports of miracles. In a similar vein John W. Montgomery asserts that the New Testament documents can be relied on to give us an accurate picture of Jesus Christ, again in substantial part because of the external historical evidence that confirms them.[3] He cites the archaeological and geographical investigations of Sir William Ramsey, which confirm the claims of Luke's gospel on ordinary events.[4] Montgomery leaves his reader with the impression that the authenticity of the miracle stories in the New Testament is secured by the authors having been found to be accurate in their ordinary historical claims. Gary Habermas makes a similar point in his debate with Antony Flew over the resurrection of Jesus. He observes that A.N. Sherwin-White had asserted that "the Book of Acts is virtually unquestioned by Roman historians, even in its details" and that "its historicity has been confirmed."[5] We are left with the clear suggestion that because Luke is understood to be accurate in his reports of the sorts of things that historians are generally in a position to evaluate, namely, ordinary events, his accuracy in the report of the Resurrection can be trusted. Claims similar to these can readily be found among other apologists for the biblical accounts.

In this essay I shall show that such claims are problematic. I shall consider some informal arguments that appear to have a bearing on the matter, and I shall also consider the conditions of confirming evidence that appear to be implicit in the claim. Carl Hempel introduced the discussion of conditions of confirming evidence some four decades ago, and extensive discussion of these conditions has taken place since then. I shall make reference to a number of well-known conditions as well as to others that are not part of the literature on confirming evidence.

One more comment, partly terminological, needs to be made before proceeding further. The apologists whose position is in question could be described as primarily concerned to establish only that *extraordinary events* (of a special kind) rather than *miracles* have occurred. The notion of miracle usually carries the connotation of an event that is both extraordinary and caused by God or some deity (under a suitable description). I do not think that the apologist is concerned at this stage in the argument to show that it is *God* (or a deity) who is responsible for the extraordinary events; the apologist wants primarily to argue that the reports of extraordinary events can be trusted. The apologist can treat separately the matter of the best explanation for the event. I shall confine my attention in the next three sections of this paper to the apologetic argument for the reliability of reports of extraordinary events and shall briefly discuss the problem of explanations of such events in the final section. What is interesting about the kind of extraordinary event in question is that it challenges a widely endorsed worldview; this will be discussed below.

PROBLEMS OF CONFIRMATION

Is the argument being advanced by the apologists in question designed to *establish* the authenticity of the biblical reports or is it designed only to *provide supporting evidence* for those reports? Is it designed to establish the reliability of the *reporters* or is it designed only to provide supporting evidence for the reliability of the reporters? These, I think, are some of the key questions that need to be posed in considering the apologetic position.

Now it must be admitted that different apologists might have several of these objectives (and perhaps even others) in mind in developing their argument; it is not always possible to identify all the objectives that an argument is intended to achieve. But the suggestion that the argument is designed to *establish* the authenticity of the biblical reports of miracles is not very plausible; it is certainly an uncharitable interpretation of the argument, for the accuracy of claims as remarkable as those alleging miracles could hardly be definitively established simply by discovering that the rather ordinary claims surrounding them are in fact accurate. Much more charitable is the position that the apologetic argument seeks to *provide supporting evidence* for the biblical reports. To employ the well-known distinction used in confirmation theory, it is much more reasonable to construe the argument as one that seeks to offer confirming evidence for the extraordinary events in the sense of "making firmer" (that is, weakly confirming) than in the sense of "making firm" (that is, strongly confirming). I will adopt the more charitable interpretation, although I will not deny that some proponents of the argument might think that accuracy in ordinary matters might establish accuracy in extraordinary ones.

But a question might be raised concerning the reporters themselves. Perhaps the main objective is to argue for the reliability of the *reporters* rather than for the accuracy of the *reports*, and some of the statements made by defenders of the argument (including some of its proponents quoted above) might lend themselves to such an interpretation. It must be granted that the fact that reporters have been found to be trustworthy in the reports on which they can be checked does have a positive bearing on their trustworthiness in the reports on which they cannot be checked. But I do not think this position reflects everything that is typically intended by the apologetic position, for at least some of its proponents have wanted to address the question of the reports themselves, perhaps because the identity of the reporters is uncertain. However, the view that this argument is about the reliability of reporters rather than the accuracy of reports is important enough to be given closer attention, and I shall do so below.

But for now, consider the view that the presence of accurate reports in the biblical documents concerning ordinary events is supporting evidence for the reports of extraordinary events. This view is very plausible, but it is worth examining in detail, in my opinion, because both informal and formal arguments can be developed to cast doubt on its plausibility. The concept used here is the familiar one carefully examined some years ago by Rudolf Carnap and Carl Hempel in which a statement or hypothesis is construed as receiving an increase in credibility from supporting or weakly confirming evidence. The statement might have acquired a certain amount of credibility from other evidence or background information, but supporting or weakly confirming evidence provides an increase in credibility. It is well known that confirming evidence is problematic – as is shown by various paradoxes of confirmation, including the paradox of the ravens and the paradox involving predicates such as "grue" – so it will not be surprising that formal arguments can be developed that cast doubt on the plausibility of the apologetic view. But it is curious that informal arguments can also be developed that call the apologetic view into question. At the very least, that view should not be advanced uncritically.

In assessing the apologetic view, it is useful to consider the response to popular claims about extraterrestrial spacecraft or UFOs. A typical report of an alleged sighting includes references to two kinds of data. First of all there are the "ordinary" features of a sighting, such as references to the time, the weather conditions, the approximate location of the sighting in relation to easily recognized landmarks, the persons present, and so on. But there are also references to the extraordinary phenomena themselves, the size and shape of the spacecraft, as well as features of its behaviour such as its speed, its manoeuverability, its ability to create unusual lighting effects, and so on. It is intriguing to note that when a report about UFOs is discovered to be accurate in its ordinary features, this discovery is not by itself generally construed as supporting evidence for the accuracy of the alleged extraordinary features of that report: the existence of UFOs is generally understood to be incapable of being advanced simply on the grounds that the reports of them are accurate with respect to the ordinary items that are capable of independent authentication. The apparent cause of this epistemic failure is the discrepancy between the claim that there are spacecraft having the characteristics typical of UFOs and the theories about the nature of the universe that have gained rational acceptance. In the absence of any other grounds for endorsing the extraordinary features accompanying the report, we remain sceptical. And this epistemic response is widely considered normal.

Numerous similar arguments concerning extraordinary events could be considered, for various popular media continually "report" incredible phenomena that are greatly at variance with rational theories about the nature of the universe, but they put these phenomena in the context of ordinary events that are readily verifiable, evidently to give them an air of plausibility. It is intriguing to observe how consistently those who are trained in rational assessment reject such accounts. While I am not over-looking the possibility that such epistemic assessments could ul-timately be judged as flawed, the discussion must begin some-where. It is particularly valuable to point out that these arguments come from real life and thereby reflect actual epis-temic assessments. Whatever value might be found in examining imaginary cases in an effort to obtain epistemic assessments, there appears to be greater value in beginning with actual cases. The apologists whose argument we are considering appear to overlook the usual rational response to reports of extraordinary events that threaten a worldview but that are couched in accurate reports of ordinary events. These reports are generally regarded as not receiving evidential support.

It is of course not impossible for reports of extraordinary events that reflect a radically different worldview to become ac-ceptable. We can perhaps speculate on the conditions under which this might happen to reports of UFOs. Perhaps numerous sightings, some of which were captured on film, could provide the evidential base to remove the currently prevalent, under-standable bias against the claim that there are extraterrestrial spacecraft. A significant buttressing effect would also be pro-vided by an explanation of how the technology to make such aircraft might have developed, what hitherto unknown physical laws it is dependent upon, and so on. It is well known that when data does not fit in readily with widely received theories, it is frequently viewed with suspicion until a theory accounting for it is in place.

APOLOGETIC CONFIRMATION THEORY

The foregoing comments have been informal and have appealed implicitly to a number of conditions of weakly confirming ev-idence that have often been present in such discussions of con-firmation. I now wish to discuss in more detail some of these conditions of confirmation, thereby defending my reservations about the apologetic position. While I will concede that there is disagreement among confirmation theorists concerning the plausibility of some conditions of confirmation, this disagree-ment should not obscure the consensus that has developed. In any event, the results obtained here will be found to be quite definitive. I will outline in this section of the paper the conditions of confirmation apparently endorsed by the apologetic position under discussion, and in the next section of the paper I will examine the plausibility of the conditions of confirmation identified here.

The apologetic thesis at stake appears to assert that confirmation of the ordinary features of a report is confirmation of the whole report, including the extraordinary features of it. It can be formally stated as follows: If evidence E (such as archaeological discoveries or independent historical data) confirms the ordinary feature O of a whole report R, then E confirms the whole report R, and E also confirms the extraordinary or unusual feature U in R.[6] This statement can be written more succinctly as follows:

If E confirms O, and R is logically equivalent to $O \& U$, then E confirms R and E also confirms U. (Condition 1)

This condition of confirmation has not been discussed in the literature or formally named, to my knowledge, so I shall refer to it simply as Condition 1. It naturally divides into the following two conditions:

If E confirms O, and R is logically equivalent to $O \& U$, then E confirms R (Condition 1a)

and

If E confirms O, and R is logically equivalent to $O \& U$, then E confirms U (Condition 1b).

I shall consider below the plausibility of these two possible conditions of confirmation.

Since neither of the two conditions appears to be present in recent discussions of confirmation, a critic might suggest that I am not doing justice to the apologist's position. To avoid this objection I shall briefly explore the possibility that the apologist in question has other conditions of confirmation in mind, conditions that have figured in recent discussions of confirmation. The major change in the interpretation of the conditions that follows is that the whole report R is construed as *entailing* its constitutive parts O and U rather than being *equivalent* to O&U. This change in the way in which the relationship between R, on the one hand, and O and U, on the other, is understood will allow us to consider the possibility that the apologist is endorsing some fairly widely entertained conditions of confirmation.

It might be suggested that the apologist is advancing the position that since O is part of the whole report R, any confirming evidence for O is also confirming evidence for R, and, moreover, whatever confirms R also confirms any logical implication of R, including the unusual report U. The position just expressed is reflected in the following pair of confirmation conditions:

If evidence E confirms a report O, and the whole report R entails O, then E confirms R (Condition 2)

and

If evidence E confirms R, then since R entails the unusual report U, E confirms U (Condition 3).

Condition 2 is commonly known as the converse consequence condition. The epistemic relation presented in this condition asserts that confirming evidence for a claim is also confirming evidence for a larger theory in which that claim is found. So confirming evidence for Newton's law of the pendulum, for instance, is also confirming evidence for the whole Newtonian theory of gravitation from which the law of the pendulum is derivable.[7] The converse consequence condition has enjoyed some support, but serious questions have also been raised concerning it. Condition 3 is the well-known special consequence condition, which has had considerable support. It asserts that evidence for a general theory is also support for the implications of that theory. It has been thought, for example, that evidential support for Newtonian physics in general is also support for the law of the pendulum and the law of the inclined plane, both of which are derivable from the more general theory.

An objector might again contend that I have not captured the intent of the apologist, and might suggest that it is not the combination of Condition 2 and Condition 3 that is being endorsed but another condition, either by itself or in conjunction with one of the conditions just named. The idea behind this third proposal is that confirming evidence for the reports of ordinary events is confirming evidence for the reports of extraordinary events, since the whole report entails both the reports of ordinary events and the reports of extraordinary events. This can be more formally stated as follows:

If evidence E confirms O, then since R entails O and R also entails U, E confirms U (Condition 4).

I am not suggesting that this hitherto unknown condition of confirming evidence is very plausible; I am simply attempting to canvass the various conditions that an apologist might be advancing.

The foregoing discussion can be summed up as follows. The apologetic thesis at stake could be interpreted as endorsing various conditions of confirmation, including certain conjunctions of those conditions, namely,

1 Condition 1a and Condition 1b, or
2 Condition 2 and Condition 3, or
3 Condition 4, or
4 Condition 4 in conjunction with Condition 2 or Condition 3.

This list does not of course exhaust the logical possibilities, but it does canvass, I suggest, the plausible and just barely plausible interpretations of the condition of confirmation implicit in the position of the apologist in question. It now remains to assess these conditions.

EVALUATING THE APOLOGIST'S CONFIRMATION THEORY

Confirmation conditions have been evaluated in various ways. The support for these conditions has come largely from their conforming to intuitively plausible assessments of confirmation conditions between particular evidence reports and particular theories. The activity of the scientific community, for instance, has been canvassed, and when a particular kind of confirmation relation receives widespread support, it is treated as prima facie plausible. But establishing confirmation conditions is far from straightforward, since it is not difficult to spot supplementary inductive arguments that are used to give confirmation conditions some much needed credibility. Undermining confirmation conditions, on the other hand, is often more straightforward, for a condition may lead to counterintuitive results on its own or, more likely, it may lead to such results in conjunction with another plausible condition of confirmation. I shall first examine the conditions of confirmation associated with the strict interpretation of Condition 1, namely, Condition 1a and Condition 1b.

There is a plausible and widely endorsed condition of confirmation that in conjunction with Condition 1a leads to counterintuitive results, namely, the Entailment Condition, which is as follows:

If evidence E entails a statement S, then E is confirming evidence for S.

The central idea behind this condition is that if an evidence report has at least as much content as another statement (so that the latter is deducible from the former), then that evidence report should also be regarded as providing confirming evidence for that deduced statement. The formal proof for the counterintuitive results is as follows:[8]

Proof 1

Step	*Justification*
(a) E entails (E or H)	Theorem of logic
(b) Thus E confirms (E or H)	Entailment Condition
(c) H is equivalent to (E or H) & (not-E or H)	Theorem of logic
(d) Thus E confirms H	Condition 1a on (b)&(c).

The implication of this demonstration is quite devastating, for since E and H are any statements whatever, it implies that any statement is confirming evidence for any other statement whatever. Endorsing Condition 1a as well as the Entailment Condition is clearly impossible.

But there are also difficulties with Condition 1b. In conjunction with the very simple supposition that some evidence report E confirms some statement H, Condition 1b leads to the highly counterintuitive result that E is confirming evidence for its own denial. The proof is as follows:

Proof 2

Step	Justification
(a) E confirms H	Supposition
(b) $(H \& not\text{-}E)$ is equivalent to $(not\text{-}E \& H)$	Theorem of logic
(c) Thus E confirms $not\text{-}E$	Condition 1b on (a)&(b).

The fact that Condition 1b allows one to deduce that a statement E is evidence of its own denial from the simple claim that E confirms some other claim H is sufficient to reject Condition 1b outright. I conclude then that the conditions of confirmation that result from a strict interpretation of the supposed confirmation relation between a whole report R and its parts O and U are untenable.

It remains now to consider the three conditions of confirmation suggested as alternatives to Condition 1a and Condition 1b. The first possibility to consider is the combination of Condition 2 and Condition 3, that is, the converse consequence condition and the special consequence condition. Hempel showed, however, that these two conditions can not be plausibly advanced. The proof that I supply requires, again, only the simple supposition that some statement E confirms some other statement H.

Proof 3

Step	Justification
(a) E confirms H	Supposition
(b) $(H \& not\text{-}E)$ entails H	Theorem of logic
(c) Thus E confirms $(H \& not\text{-}E)$	Condition 2 on (a) & (b)

(d) (H & not-E) entails not-E   Theorem of logic
(e) Thus E confirms not-E   Condition 3 on (c) & (d).

The counterintuitive result that any statement E confirms its denial on the supposition that there is some H that E confirms,
makes it impossible to endorse both Condition 2 and Condition
3.

There is one remaining condition that needs to be examined,
and that is Condition 4. This condition can also be shown to
lead to implausible results, again on the supposition that some
E confirms some H.

Proof 4

Step   *Justification*
(a) E confirms H   Supposition
(b) not-E & H entails H   Theorem of logic
(c) not-E & H entails not-E   Theorem of logic
(d) E confirms not-E   Condition 4 on (a) – (c).

This result again shows that Condition 4 cannot be plausibly
maintained, either by itself or with other suggested conditions
of confirmation.

The position of the apologist in question can now be summarized. I have said that the apologist's claims about confirming
evidence amount to endorsing (1) Condition 1a and Condition
1b or (2) Condition 2 and Condition 3 or (3) Condition 4 or
(4) Condition 4 in conjunction with either Condition 2 or Condition 3. I have shown that Condition 1a is inconsistent with
the highly plausible entailment condition, that Condition 1b is
implausible by itself, that Condition 2 and Condition 3 cannot
be maintained together, and that Condition 4 is implausible by
itself. I conclude therefore that the position on confirmation evidently (or possibly) advanced by the apologists in question cannot be plausibly maintained.

POSSIBLE REPLIES

There are various replies that an apologist for the authenticity
of the biblical reports of miracles might wish to make at this

point. A possible but implausible response is that the apologist in fact employs a strong concept of confirmation rather than a weak concept. I argued above that such an interpretation of the apologist's position is not a charitable one, but more formal grounds can be advanced for setting it aside.9

I wish to consider another response here that I alluded to earlier in this chapter, namely, that the apologist's position is that if a *reporter* can be trusted about the ordinary part of a report, then s/he can be trusted about the extraordinary part as well.

I would say first of all, in reply, that this interpretation of the apologist's claim overlooks the fact that we can and do make independent assessments of the credibility of reporters and of the epistemic relationship between statements. It appears that most of the apologists for the New Testament documents have wanted to speak about the statements themselves, not just about the persons making the statements, especially since there is often some uncertainty about who is responsible for the documents in their present form. The resurrection of Jesus, for instance, is reported by all the gospels – whoever their original authors and later editors might have been – and it is these reports that are in question. Since we are not able to settle issues of authorship so long after the fact, we are forced to consider the statements that have been made and the epistemic relationships that we can discover between them. Moreover, if the purpose of the argument is to show that an author is reliable, that is only because the author's reliability might provide a way of getting to the credibility of the reports of extraordinary events. This interpretion of the apologetic position inserts an extra step about the general credibility of the reporter, but only in order to be able to say that there is supporting evidence for the report of the extraordinary event.

The fact remains that a reporter might be trustworthy in connection with ordinary phenomena but not generally credible, for a reporter might be misled or deceived about the extraordinary events that s/he is reporting. Or s/he might be uncritically committed to a worldview consistent with extraordinary claims. The possibility of being misled or deceived appears to be exacerbated when there is a considerable time gap between events and the reports of them, for example, the approximately thirty years that is generally considered the minimum time between the miracles alleged of Jesus and the reports of them in the gospels. There is plenty of room in such circumstances for error, including perceptual errors, mistaken memories, exaggeration in oral transmissions between original participants in events and the final reporters, the possible influence of a supernaturalistic worldview on someone attempting to "objectively report" data, and so on. It is plausible that a reporter who is fully capable of handling events that are part of the ordinary scheme of things fails to do justice to events of an extraordinary kind, and not because of a penchant for deceit and fraud, but because of the much more complex character of the kind of extraordinary events alleged. Consider the account in Luke 8 of Jesus bringing back to life the child of one of the rulers of a synagogue (also found in Mark 5 and Matthew 9). The obvious problems include the fact that at least thirty years elapsed between the alleged event and the account, that Luke was not present on the occasion, according to the account attributed to him, that the supposed resurrection was witnessed by only six people, and that no explanation is given for thinking that the child was dead rather than in a coma. In questioning the reliability of the reporter we are not questioning his attempt to get the facts correct – Luke might have done as conscientious a job in researching relevant information about the alleged resurrection as he evidently did in connection with ordinary facts. But conscientiousness in securing information about the alleged miracle does not automatically confer reliability on the reporter, and thus the conscientiousness of the reporter does not provide confirming evidence in favour of the report of the miracle. There are too many ways in which a scrupulous and sincere investigator might be misled. So the digression by way of the reporter does not appear to be a helpful strategy.

Perhaps this last point can be reinforced by considering allegations of miracles made in our own day, using a time period comparable to the period commonly accepted as separating the alleged miracles of Jesus and the reports of them in the gospels. Consider a document written in 1991 about one of the faith healers well known to American culture at the present time, Oral Roberts for instance, that alleges an instantaneous healing of some very obvious physical malady around 1960. Suppose that this document includes comments about ordinary features of American life including commentary about leading political figures and events, all of which are accurate within standards accepted by historians. Does the apparent trustworthiness of the writer on ordinary matters confer trustworthiness on the writer in general, thereby conferring weak confirmation on the report of the alleged miracle? It is interesting to observe that such allegations of miracles made in our day are not widely accepted, particularly in that part of the scholarly community that is committed to determining which beliefs are rationally credible and that constantly assesses epistemic claims. This assessment of miracles is commonly made in spite of the fact that such reports might be offered by otherwise reliable reporters and are presented along with largely accurate reports of an ordinary sort. Perhaps the problem could be described this way: while we ordinarily grant that the trustworthiness of a reporter on items that we can independently verify provides confirming evidence that the reporter is generally trustworthy (not strong but weak confirming evidence, although it might be considerable in certain circumstances), such confirming evidence is not conveyed to every report.[10] The epistemic principle asserting that trustworthiness on ordinary matters transfers to extraordinary matters proves too much, for if it were to be embraced, many more of us would accept contemporary reports of religious miracles, of UFOs, and the like. I submit that the epistemic principle that concentrates attention on the reliability of a reporter is not helpful.

There is another objection that should be considered, namely, that the argument against the apologetic position proves too much. It might be thought that all reports of extraordinary events, including events examined by ordinary science, must be discounted if the only evidence for them is the accuracy of the reports of ordinary events occurring in conjunction with the reports of extraordinary events. It might be thought, for instance, that the argument I have developed would require the rejection of a report of the existence of an extraordinary plant if the only basis for the report is the discovery of a book on plants that reports the existence of the extraordinary plant as well as other plants that are well known and found to be accurately described. This objection is an important one, for it raises a pivotal problem with the kinds of phenomena under consideration in this chapter.

It is apparent that the reports of UFOs and of miracles of the biblical sort do not mesh well with well-established belief systems and bodies of scientific knowledge. I am not saying that they explicitly contradict those belief systems or bodies of knowledge; they might do so, but that would need to be shown in detail with an alleged case of contradiction. To embrace reports of events such as the biblical miracles requires a serious expansion of the whole scientific framework within which events are fitted. To accept the report of an unusual plant, for example, the first report of a plant capable of trapping and consuming insects, does not require a substantial revision of the framework for botany, but to accept a report of a dead body being resurrected or a stormy sea calmed by a command does require such a revision. It is apparent that the kind of extraordinary event under discussion does not fit into well-established belief systems or bodies of scientific knowledge. Events of this kind cannot be authenticated, I maintain, by a discovery that the reports of the ordinary events associated with them are found to be accurate.

It might be thought that the sceptical victory I have achieved to this point, if my argument is cogent, is a rather easy one because of the general climate of scepticism towards miracles that can be readily found in philosophical circles. I shall venture then to conclude this paper with a few remarks on the kind of argument an apologist might consider for the historicity of the kind of extraordinary events in question. The most formidable intellectual obstacle to accepting the historicity of the biblical documents in their reports of extraordinary events is of course the suspicion that the kind of universe depicted in these documents just does not exist. It is hard to accept as historically authentic documents that suggest that alongside ordinary men and women there are "gods and demigods and heroes"[11] who can raise the dead, turn water into wine, call down fire from the heavens, walk on water, strike opponents with blindness, and so on. The suggestion that the Bible comes from a non-scientific age in which the universe was viewed as populated by strange beings or by people with strange powers is very difficult to reject for people reared in a context dominated by science.

I suggest that the apologetic that is needed would show that at least some kinds of events alleged in the biblical documents are still found today. A small number of well-documented cases of healing or multiplication of food or fire falling from heaven (or what appears to be fire) and so on, or perhaps a large number of reasonably well-documented cases, could begin to undermine the intellectual bias that people commonly and understandably have against the historicity of the biblical documents. In short, the inadequacy of current belief systems and the need to consider alternative or additional belief systems needs to be shown by drawing attention to the probable occurrence of anomalous cases. While the events alleged by the biblical writers might not have to be *repeatable*, that is, capable of being repeated at will under experimental conditions, in order to be believable, it does seem reasonable to require them to be *repeated*. Of course, showing that an extraordinary event has occurred is one thing, and providing convincing grounds for thinking that God (or a deity) was involved is quite another.

If events similar to those reported in the miracle stories in the Bible were to be found at the present time, the credibility of those ancient documents would be enhanced. Accounts that had been dismissed as fictitious or merely mythological would again come under scrutiny. A similar situation would probably occur, I suggest, if a definitive sighting and subsequent examination of a UFO were to take place. Documents that currently lie in limbo would be revived and canvassed for further clues about the nature of extraterrestrial life.

The situation with the biblical miracles is comparable to the current situation surrounding reports of UFOs. The ordinary historical events reported by the biblical writers might be believable enough, especially if they are corroborated by other historical material; but the reports of the miraculous defy belief. While I am not suggesting that the biblical writers deliberately set out to deceive their readers, it is surely possible that they were somehow misled or taken in. In the absence either of an internationally accredited body of scrutinizers ascertaining that extraordinary phenomena did indeed take place, or of a sizeable body of similar phenomena reported in different places by various people over a significant period of time, a critic of the biblical documents is surely not irrational in doubting the authenticity of the miraculous, all the while granting the accuracy of the documents inasmuch as they detail ordinary historical phenomena.

I conclude then that the apologist's claim examined above is questionable. On the basis of informal and formal arguments, I have suggested that the credibility of claims of miraculous or extraordinary events cannot be plausibly considered to rest on the accuracy of such things as ordinary historical, geographical, and archaeological reports. I have suggested another approach that an apologist might consider, and in doing so I have implied another possible principle of confirmation. But its scrutiny is a task for another occasion.[12]

APPENDIX

The strong interpretation of the apologist's position asserts that evidence that "makes firm" reports of ordinary events also makes firm the whole report, including the reports of extraordinary events. This interpretation can be more formally expressed as follows:

> If E strongly confirms O and R is logically equivalent to O & U, then E strongly confirms R (Condition 5)

and

> If E strongly confirms O and R is logically equivalent to O & U, then E strongly confirms U (Condition 6).

These claims have a prima facie implausibility, and examples will show their inadequacy.

A question arises concerning an appropriate interpretation of the concept of strong confirmation. Many theorists, but not all, have endorsed the view that it satisfies the axioms of the probability calculus. If we assume it does, then we can express the two conditions as follows:

> If $p(O, E) = 1$ and R is logically equivalent to O & U, then $p(O\&U, E) = 1$ (Condition 5')

and

> If $p(O, E) = 1$ and R is logically equivalent to O & U, then $p(U, E) = 1$ (Condition 6').

The inadmissibility of these conditions can now be shown using a simple example. Let $O = Fa$, $E = Fa$ & Fb, $R = Fa$ & Fc, and $U = Fc$. In these circumstances $p(O, E) = 1$; R is logically equivalent to O & U; but $p(O\&U, E) = 1$, for $p(O\&U, E)$ is $p(Fa$ & Fc, Fa & $Fb)$ and Fc is independent of Fb. This shows that Condition 5' cannot be satisfied. Using the same assignments for O, E, R, and U as above, one can show that $p(O, E) = 1$ and R is logically equivalent to $O\&U$, but $p(U, E) = 1$, for $p(U, E)$ is $p(Fc, Fa$ & $Fb)$. This shows the inadmissibility of Condition 6'.

While it is more difficult to assess the situation if the concept of strong confirmation is thought not to satisfy the probability calculus, examples similar to the ones just used show their implausibility. All that is required is the admission that Fa & Fb strongly confirms Fa and that Fa & Fb strongly confirms neither Fa & Fc nor Fc. This is sufficient to shift the onus of proof onto the would-be defender of the apologetic position that the concept of strong confirmation might be used here.

NOTES

1 Gary Habermas makes reference to a number of these grounds in his exchange with Antony Flew over the alleged resurrection of Jesus. See Terry L. Miethe, ed., *Did Jesus Rise from the Dead: The Resurrection Debate* (San Francisco: Harper & Row 1987).

2 F.F. Bruce, *The New Testament Documents: Are They Reliable?* rev. ed. (Downers Grove, IL: Intervarsity Press 1960), 62.

3 John W. Montgomery, *History and Christianity* (Downers Grove, IL: Intervarsity Press 1964), 40.

4 Ibid., 31.

5 Miethe, *Resurrection Debate*, 58.

6 I use a two-termed concept of confirmation in the discussion that follows. The concept could be relativized to background information, but that would not change the results obtained.

7 There is an important difference between the Newtonian theory of gravitation and the law of the pendulum, on the one hand, and a whole report R and its unusual component U, on the other, for the law of the pendulum is a special case of the Newtonian theory, while U is not a special case of R.

8 Carl G. Hempel was one of the earliest confirmation theorists to discuss various conditions of confirmation in the weak sense of "to

confirm" (meaning something like "to make firmer"), which is the
sense being discussed in this paper. His "Studies in the Logic of
Confirmation" was first published in *Mind*, 54 (1945), 1–26, 97–121,
and contains the kind of proof given here. *Proof 3* is drawn from his
work, and I am indebted in other ways to his work on confirmation
theory.

9 Rudolf Carnap distinguished these two senses in the preface to the
second edition of *Logical Foundations of Probability* (Chicago: University
of Chicago Press 1962). Interpreting the apologist's position using
the strong sense would be to assert that evidence that makes firm
the ordinary reports also makes firm the whole report, including
the reports of extraordinary events. This position is examined in
the appendix to this chapter.

10 There is a principle here that is a variant on what has been called
the transitivity condition of (weak) confirmation, which asserts that
if E confirms F and F confirms G, then E confirms G. Wesley
Salmon offered an informal argument for its inadequacy in "Consistency, Transitivity, and Inductive Support," *Ratio* 7 (1965), 164–9.
The example he used was as follows. The report that Joe McQuarie
lives in Gnaw Bone, Indiana is (weakly) confirming evidence that
Joe McQuarie speaks English, and the report that Joe McQuarie
speaks English is (weakly) confirming evidence that Joe McQuarie
does not live in Indiana, but of course the report that Joe McQuarie
lives in Gnaw Bone, Indiana is not (weakly) confirming evidence
that he does not live in Indiana. I am not suggesting that the epistemic principle making reference to a reporter is precisely captured
by the condition just stated, but I do think that something closely
resembling a transitivity condition is implicit in it.

11 I have drawn this phrase from Plato's *Apology* 28.

12 I acknowledge the useful comments of William Alston, Robert
Larmer, Hugo Meynell, and several anonymous referees on earlier
versions of this paper.

14 Miracles and Testimony: A Reply to Wiebe

ROBERT LARMER

In chapter 13, Phillip Wiebe attacks the argument that the biblical reports of miracles gain substantial credence from the fact that the biblical writers have been found to be accurate in their reports of ordinary historical events. His method is to demonstrate, both by informal arguments from analogy and formal arguments based on confirmation theory, that accurate propositions concerning ordinary events in no way imply or render plausible the accuracy of statements concerning extraordinary events. I am not persuaded, however, that he has done justice to the argument he is attacking.

First, even without diagnosing precisely where it goes wrong, it appears that Wiebe's argument, not unlike Hume's, is in danger of refuting itself by proving too strong. If successful, it seems to rule out not only biblical miracles but a host of other commonly accepted historical events. By way of example, consider Hannibal's crossing the Alps to attack the Romans from the rear. This seems to qualify as an extraordinary, historically unique event that cannot be established except on the basis of testimonial evidence. If we inquire why the testimony that establishes this event should be trusted, the answer will be that it comes from sources that have proven to be reliable in reporting ordinary historical events. However, applying Wiebe's argument, we will be forced to recognize that this reliability constitutes no justification for believing that Hannibal crossed the Alps, since the accuracy of testimony concerning ordinary events in no way implies or makes plausible the accuracy of testimony concerning extraordinary events. Realizing this, we will give up the obviously unjustified belief that Hannibal crossed the Alps and turn to some form of "higher criticism" whereby we attempt to explain how such mythological elements crept into Roman beliefs. Nor will our problem be limited to such straightforwardly historical claims. As C.D. Broad long ago pointed out, unless testimony is sufficient to justify at least a tentative belief in unusual events, it is hard to see how science could ever progress, since progress is often achieved precisely by taking into account testimony concerning unusual and, at least at the moment, theoretically intractable events.[1]

I have been suggesting that Wiebe's argument falls victim to a form of reductio ad absurdum insofar as it proves too much. Wiebe, however, is aware of this objection and feels that it can be met. I am not persuaded that Wiebe does in fact meet it, but rather than press the strategy of reductio, I propose to offer a more direct analysis of where his argument goes wrong.

I shall proceed not by criticizing his use of confirmation theory but by criticizing his informal arguments from analogy. My justification for proceeding in this manner is twofold. First, as Wiebe admits, theoretical accounts of the nature of confirming evidence are widely admitted to be problematic. Second, it seems that the force of his argument rests largely on his analogy concerning UFOs. We might well be persuaded that the absence of a theoretical account of confirming evidence is not very threatening to belief either in miracles or scientific claims if we all judge these beliefs to be rational. If we become persuaded, however, that the considerations advanced to justify belief in miracles would also force us to regard belief in UFOs as justified, we are liable to conclude that such considerations constitute no evidence for miracles.

Let me begin by making two very general points. The first is that unless one witnesses the unusual event oneself, testimonial evidence is essential to establish the occurrence of unusual events. This is an obvious point, but I do not think Wiebe has appreciated its full significance. In his UFO example he suggests that we could accept the claim that UFOs exist if we captured one and if a broad, internationally based group of experts established that human technology could not have produced the machine in question. I agree that this would make belief in UFOs acceptable, but the reason would not be that we would have dispensed with the necessity of testimonial evidence. Insisting that we dispense with testimonial evidence would have the curious consequence that in order to believe in UFOs, one must not only capture a UFO oneself, but must oneself *be* a broad, internationally based group of experts!

The second general point is that the only way we in fact have of evaluating the reliability of a witness's testimony concerning extraordinary events is to evaluate the reliability of that witness's testimony concerning events that admit of external support. Again, this seems an obvious point, but, again, I do not think Wiebe has appreciated its full significance. Unless the members of Wiebe's broad, internationally based group of experts can trust one another's testimony, how are they to arrive at the conclusion that human technology is not sufficiently advanced to produce the machine in question? Unless we can trust the testimony of these experts, how are we laypersons to believe the results of their investigation? Since neither science nor history can dispense with testimonial evidence, and since the only way of evaluating the reliability of a witness's testimony concerning extraordinary events is to evaluate the accuracy of her testimony on matters that admit of external support, it is clear that Wiebe is wrong to claim that the reliability of the biblical writers on ordinary matters is irrelevant to the question of whether their reports of miracles are trustworthy.

How, then, does Wiebe's argument go wrong. I suggest in at least two ways. First, it seems that he has misrepresented the argument he wishes to criticize. The focus of the argument is not on the logical relation between various propositions but on the trustworthiness of a particular individual's testimony. Attempting to apply confirmation theory misses the point that what is at issue is not whether certain propositions about ordinary events logically imply certain propositions about extraordinary events[2] but whether a reporter whose testimony can be trusted concerning the ordinary features of an event has a strong claim to be trustworthy in her testimony concerning the extraordinary features of an event.

Wiebe considers this possibility but rejects it on three grounds. The first is that in many cases the authors/editors of the New Testament documents are unknown and that there is little extra-biblical historical information on which to evaluate them. The second is that although a reporter might be trustworthy in connnection with ordinary phenomena, s/he might be deceived or misled with regard to extraordinary events. The third is that this argument proves too much, since the epistemic principle that transfers trustworthiness on ordinary matters over to extraordinary matters would force us to accept reports of UFOs and contemporary religious miracles.

Against Wiebe's first reason I would argue that although we may not know the name of the author/editor of a document, we are scarcely precluded from assessing whether he or she has been accurate in reporting ordinary events. Neither is the extra-biblical historical information so lacking that we cannot evaluate the accuracy of the biblical writers in recording ordinary events. As Wiebe himself notes, Roman historians have found the New Testament writers correct on numerous historical matters, so much so that they consider them valuable historical sources.

Wiebe's second ground for rejection is based on his claim that the sincerity and scrupulousness of the biblical writers in accurately reporting ordinary facts does not guarantee the accuracy of their reports concerning extraordinary facts, since it is always possible that they were misled by their sources, by their own perceptual abilities, or by a lack of discrimination in evaluating evidence. This claim may be true, but it seems to assume that it is invariably a simple matter to be correct about ordinary events and invariably a difficult matter to be correct about extraordinary events. I suggest that this is a very questionable assumption on both counts.

Consider, by way of example, Luke's report of "ordinary" facts concerning chronology and the use of official titles and his report of the extraordinary fact of Paul healing a man who had been lame from birth and never walked (Acts 14:9,10). It is no easy matter to be correct on these ordinary facts of chronology and protocol, yet Luke has been proven accurate time and time again. Indeed, it seems that it would be a lot easier for him to be mistaken on these matters than on his testimony concerning Paul's miracle. Luke travelled with Paul and had every opportunity to evaluate whether Paul was prone to exaggeration, he was in contact with men and women who would have witnessed the event, and last, but certainly not least, it seems probable that he would have had opportunities to meet with the man who had been healed. Unless we are prepared to charge Luke with dishonesty, it seems that the accuracy that he displays in the far more difficult matters of correctly reporting proper chronology and official protocol is a strong reason to trust his report concerning unusual events with which he had direct involvement.

What Wiebe fails to appreciate is that the difficulties inherent in accurately reporting extraordinary events are equally inherent in accurately reporting ordinary events. All sorts of ordinary events, to use his words, give "plenty of room ... for ... perceptual errors, mistaken memories, exaggeration ... between original participants in events and the final reporters, [and] the possible influence of a ... worldview on one attempting to 'objectively report' data." It seems, therefore, that if a person can be trusted to overcome these obstacles in accurately reporting ordinary events, there is good reason to believe she can be trusted to overcome these obstacles in accurately reporting extraordinary events.

Wiebe's failure to see this vitiates his discussion of Luke's account of Jesus bringing Jairus' daughter back to life. He seems to accept that testimonial evidence can establish the "ordinary" details of the incident, for example that Jairus had a daughter who was very ill, that he approached Jesus for help, that Jesus agreed to come but was delayed on his way, that while they were on their way someone came and reported that Jairus' daughter was dead, that Jesus reassured Jairus that his daughter would be healed, and that the daughter's regaining consciousness coincided with Jesus' visit to her sickbed. What Wiebe does not feel the testimonial evidence can establish is that the daughter was dead rather than in a coma and hence that an extraordinary event really occurred.

Suppose, however, we grant that there is not sufficient reason to believe that the girl was dead, rather than in a coma. Have we really done away with extraordinary events? It does not seem so, since we must still explain Jesus' absolute assurance that he could heal the girl, even though, to the best of his knowledge, she was dead. This, in itself, is an extraordinary event that needs explanation. Suppose, then, we excise this event from the report. Have we now done away with extraordinary events? It seems not, since we have an extraordinary event as the cause of Jesus being delayed, namely his healing of the woman with the issue of blood. Suppose we eliminate this fantastic element from the narrative. Are we finally free of the extraordinary? It seems not, since it was Jesus' alleged ability to heal that led Jairus to approach him in the first place. Eliminating this, however, leaves us not with a historical core of ordinary events but with nothing at all. It seems, therefore, that unless there is reason to accept the extraordinary elements of this story as historical, there is no reason to accept the ordinary elements as historical.

My point is that the natural and supernatural or, if you prefer, ordinary and extraordinary, are so remarkably intertwined in the New Testament that there can be no question of accepting its testimony concerning ordinary events, yet rejecting its testimony concerning extraordinary events.[3] I do not have time to argue this in detail, but those who doubt me would do well to retrace the steps of the liberal quest to get behind the New Testament documents and uncover the real, that is, non-miracle working Jesus. Since criticism revealed no time at which accounts of Jesus did not include extraordinary events, it was concluded that we can have little or no knowledge of the historical Jesus. I would argue that this is an absurd conclusion, but it does make clear that we cannot disentangle the supernatural and natural in the New Testament. The ultimate consequence of Wiebe's position is not to take us to the historical core of the New Testament but rather to disregard its claim to be a historical document.

Wiebe's third claim is that the argument proves too much, for it would force us to accept not only that there is strong support for biblical miracles but also strong support for contemporary reports of religious miracles and reports of UFOs. This assertion seems suspiciously a priori in the absence of any detailed comparison of the bodies of testimonial evidence for these events. It is also a somewhat puzzling claim, since I know through conversations with him that Wiebe accepts, as do I, the continuing occurrence of miracles in the twentieth century. Regarding reports of UFOs, I am not persuaded there is the quality of testimonial evidence that we have for the biblical miracles or for some contemporary miracles.⁴ What I do not feel free to do is to reject testimony regarding UFOs solely on the ground that it reports something extraordinary. As already noted, testimony can be distorted by perceptual error, mistaken memory, exaggerated accounts, or even outright deceit, but this is a hazard in the reporting not simply of extraordinary but also of ordinary events. Any rejection of an account of a miracle or UFO should be based on evidence that one of these factors has indeed distorted testimony. Rejecting testimonial evidence for miracles or UFOs simply on the basis that it reports miracles or UFOs amounts to begging the question.

The second way in which Wiebe's argument goes wrong is that he uncritically accepts that belief in miracles conflicts with a scientific understanding of the universe. He suggests that "The most formidable intellectual obstacle to accepting the historicity of the biblical documents in their reports of extraordinary events is ... the suspicion that the kind of universe depicted in these documents just does not exist. It is hard to accept documents as historically authentic that suggest that alongside ordinary men and women there are 'gods and demigods and heroes' [Plato's Apology 28] who can raise the dead, turn water into wine, call down fire from the heavens, walk on water, strike opponents with blindness, and so on." Indeed, this view that miracles clash with scientific knowledge underlies his rejection of the claim that the accuracy of a reporter concerning ordinary events provides reason to trust the accuracy of the reporter with regard to extraordinary events. In normal circumstances, he is quite prepared to grant that "the trustworthiness of a reporter on items we can independently verify provides confirming evidence that the reporter is generally trustworthy" and that such evidence might be of considerable strength. It is only in the case of events that do not mesh with established belief systems and bodies of scientific knowledge that he refuses to take into account the trustworthiness of a reporter concerning independently verifiable events.

In response, several points deserve mention. First, the facile rejection of what on other grounds would be considered reliable testimony, fails to do justice to the fact that science, no less than history, relies on "plain witnessing" and any attempt to escape this reliance is bound to fail. The business of science is not to legislate what can happen but rather to try and explain what has happened.

Two examples worth pondering in this regard are provided by Stanley Jaki:

Characteristic of the stubborn resistance of scientific academies to ... [reports of meteors] was Laplace's shouting, "We've had enough such myths," when Pictet, a fellow academician, urged a reconsideration of the evidence provided by "lay-people" as plain eyewitnesses. [In a foot- note Jaki records that during the decades of the Enlightenment, the resistance of those Academies, influenced largely by the Académie des Sciences in Paris, became so great as to result in the discarding of all meteorites from museums] Laymen were they in the sense that they had no telescopes, no training in celestial mechanics, no knowledge of trajectories, the azimuth, right and left ascension. But they could register with absolute certainty that a fiery body had just hit the ground nearby and could unerringly distinguish its still warm stony remains as something not belonging to the soil around it. That such a kind of witnessing stands in its own right was the point recognized by a doctor on being confronted with the objection of a colleague who in- sisted that the wide-open fracture below the left knee of Pieter De Rudder (1822–1898), the subject of possibly the most startling cure related to Lourdes, could not be accepted for a fact because the two ends of the broken bone protruding through the skin had not been certified by a medical commission. The reply of that rightly indignant physician, "it does not take a tailor to see that a coat is full of holes," contains an instructiveness that is practically inexhaustible.[5]

Second, I see no reason to grant that belief in miracles conflicts with scientific understanding. Wiebe writes that "to embrace re- ports of such events as the biblical miracles requires a serious expansion of the whole scientific framework within which events are fitted." This is simply false. I have shown in detail elsewhere that miracles considered as events produced by God's supernat- ural intervention can occur without violating any laws of nature.[6] God, by creating or destroying the stuff of nature, that is, mass/ energy, to which the laws apply, can create within nature events that would not otherwise occur, without violating or suspending any of the laws of nature. It is true, however, that the occurrence of miracles forces the abandonment of a naturalistic metaphysics in which the physical universe is seen as all that exists. Establishing the Resurrection or the Virgin Birth does not require abandoning well-evidenced theories of how physical reality behaves when it is not interfered with but rather the metaphysical view that there is nothing outside physical reality capable of intervening upon it.

Third, it is far from clear that the Bible is saturated with superstition. In the context of the present discussion, it bears pointing out that in the example, already cited, of Paul healing the man lame from birth, Paul and Barnabus took great pains to convince the crowd witnessing the miracle that they were not gods, demigods, or heroes (Acts 14:8-18). Given examples such as this, I can, perhaps, be forgiven my suspicion that contemporary willingness to discount the worth of testimonial evidence and relegate accounts of miracles to the realm of superstition and myth is based not on an actual evaluation of the evidence but rather on the assumption that miracles cannot occur.

Finally, in closing, I want to comment briefly on Wiebe's claim that what is needed, if we are take the extraordinary events recorded in the Bible seriously, is the demonstration that at least some of these types of events take place today. He suggests that if such extraordinary events were reported in many places, by many people, over a long period of time and if an internationally accredited body of scrutinizers ascertained that such extraordinary phenomena had indeed taken place in more recent times, then, and only then, the critic would be justified in accepting the testimony of the biblical writers concerning such events.

First, I agree that the occurrence in contemporary times of the same type of extraordinary events as those recorded in the Bible provides confirming evidence of those biblical events. I attend a church in which the charismatic gifts spoken of in the New Testament are practised. I have witnessed some of the same types of events that are recorded in the New Testament and know individuals who have had first-hand experience of such events. In the face of such evidence, it would be very difficult to persuade me that the biblical accounts are mythological or the product of primitive superstition.

Wiebe seems to be suggesting, however, that the occurrence of such contemporary events is required if one is to believe in the extraordinary events recorded in the Bible. This, I think, is a mistake. The occurrence of similar events in contemporary times is no more necessary for grounding a rational belief in the events recorded in the Bible than a second crossing of the Alps by a Carthaginian army is necessary to ground belief in Hannibal's exploit.

Second, Wiebe seems to set too much stock in internationally accredited bodies of scrutineers. As the examples provided by Jaki demonstrate, there is no guarantee that "expert bodies" are more objective or in a better position to establish the occurrence of the events in question than laypersons. I see no reason to doubt the sane and sober testimony of a person of good character simply on the grounds that he or she has not yet been investigated by such a body of scrutineers. When, for example, my minister, whom I know to be of good character and judgment, tells me that his father experienced an overnight recovery from the last stages of cancer that had been diagnosed as terminal by a number of doctors, and when his report is confirmed by a large number of people acquainted with his father, I feel no need to suspend belief until I can form an internationally accredited body of scrutineers. We can, if Wiebe likes, debate whether this was really a miracle, but that debate is irrelevant to our present discussion of what is required to ground a rational belief in extraordinary events.

I conclude that Wiebe has given no reason to reject the apologetic argument that the habitual accuracy of the biblical writers on ordinary matters that can be checked is a strong reason to trust their reports concerning the occurrence of extraordinary events. Both his characterization of the argument and his views concerning the type and amount of evidence required to establish a miracle are mistaken.

NOTES

1 C.D. Broad, "Hume's Theory of the Credibility of Miracles," *Proceedings of the Aristotelian Society* 17 (1916–17): 77–94.
2 Since a miracle is understood as a supernatural intervention upon the natural order, we would scarcely expect that statements about ordinary processes, that is, natural events, would logically imply

statements about extraordinary events arising from such intervention.

3 Bernard Ramm makes this point when he writes, "Older synoptic critics of a modernistic bent considered it a feasible task to go through the Gospels and shave off the miracles much like warts and leave the fabric of the record intact. For different reasons conservatives and form-critics have joined together to renounce this as an impossible effort. The miraculous is part of the very fibre of the record that cannot be cut like a superficial growth and an extraneous and imposed body of material. Miracles inhere vitally in the records themselves, and if deleted render the record unintelligible.

Around many miracles are certain events *before* and *after*. The former set the stage for the miracle, and the latter deal with the consequences that follow from it. If the miracle is pruned off, the material before and after is left dangling in midair." *Protestant Christian Evidences* (Chicago: Moody Press 1953), 137–8.

4 Following Wiebe, I am taking "UFO" to mean "extraterrestrial spacecraft."

5 Stanley L. Jaki, *Miracles and Physics* (Front Royal, VA: Christendom Press 1989) 94–5. Jaki is quoting from L. Monden, *Signs and Wonders: A Study of the Miraculous Element in Religion.* (New York: Desclee 1966), 244. A well-known philosopher of science once remarked in public debate with me that with regard to miracles, one has to choose between science and two-thousand-year-old superstition, that is, Christianity. When I commented that many of the extraordinary events reported in the New Testament are also reported as occurring in the twentieth century, he replied that we should not waste the time of scientists by investigating such reports.

6 See chapter 3 of this volume. For a fuller exposition and defense, see my book *Water Into Wine?* (Montreal: McGill-Queen's University Press 1988).

15 Miracles as Evidence Against the Existence of God

CHRISTINE OVERALL

Most recent discussions of the concept of miracle have concentrated mainly on the relationship between miracles and scientific laws.[1] As a result, I believe, there has been far too little attention paid to the alleged evidential connections between the existence of miracles and the existence of God.

One reason, presumably, that some philosophers and theologians have traditionally been interested in miracles is that it is assumed that their existence would be evidence – probably conclusive evidence – for the existence of God.[2] (And here, by "God," I mean the God of Christianity; in John Hick's definition, "the infinite, eternal, uncreated, personal reality, who has created all that exists and who is revealed to human creatures as holy and loving."[3]) Despite this assumption, I would nevertheless like to ask what I think (in light of the epistemic difficulties in providing evidence for the existence of a miracle) may be a sort of counterfactual question: namely, if miracles were to occur, just what would their occurrence really show?

In the context of the type of definition of "miracle" used recently by some philosophers, it becomes difficult to frame the question in just this way. For they appear to build in to the concept of miracle the notion that the event is brought about by a supernatural being. Douglas Odegard, for example, claims, "Some who for the sake of argument make the violation of a law a condition of being a miracle would go further and add the condition that the event must have religious significance or be produced by a god. But ... the notion of violating a law is best understood such that we cannot justifiably claim that an event is a violation unless we have good reason to believe that it is produced by a god."[4] Similarly, in discussing the concept of miracle, Ian Walker states that "the concept of violations [of natural laws], if it is to be coherent, must have a 'supernatural precondition' built into it. This means that 'violation' miracles can only be characterized on the precondition that they may be the result of a supernatural force at work."[5] And David Basinger argues that "it would be useful for theologians and philosophers to refrain from defining miracles as violations of natural laws and define them rather as permanently inexplicable or coincidental *direct acts of God*."[6]

Hence, to say that an event x is a miracle is already, by definition, to say that a supernatural being exists and that the event cannot be used as independent evidence for that being's existence. This concept of miracle, therefore, encourages us to focus on the problem of the identification of a particular event as a miracle, rather than on the exploration of the connection between a certain kind of event, called a miracle, and God. To avoid this terminological problem, in what follows I shall mean by "miracle" simply an event that is a violation of natural law or that (following Basinger)[7] is permanently inexplicable. However, regardless of what definition is adopted, the philosophical question turns out to be the same: What is the connection between, on the one hand, the existence of an event that is a violation of natural law or that is permanently inexplicable (a miracle, in my sense) and, on the other, the existence of God?

Some writers have claimed, at least, that the connection between the existence of miracles and the existence of God is not a straightforward one. Consider the following arguments.

(a) God is thought of as a being existing outside (in, of course, a non-spatial sense) space and time; he is not a part of the space-time order, but independent of it. "While it makes sense to talk about influence and interference between particular things *within* the universe, this is not the case with the whole ... One may ask in a similar vein whether the cause (God) can be otherwise if the effect (the miracle) is spatio-temporal. Moreover, a theist taking this line must explain how God can hear and answer requests (spatio-temporal events) without being in the space-time sphere himself. Yet, many miracles involve requests and answers."[8] The point here is that a violation of natural law or a permanently inexplicable event occurring within space-time is not the sort of thing that a being outside space-time could produce. The problem here is not, of course, an empirical one but a logical one. Thus the argument raises doubts about what the connection between God and miracles could possibly be.

(b)   Another problem about making a connection between miracles and God is cited by Alastair McKinnon. He points out that according to "the supernatural account," God is the cause of all events. Hence, says McKinnon, "it makes no sense to say that he is the special cause of one or more particular events."[9] McKinnon is suggesting that the believer in God cannot have it both ways: either all events are caused by God – in which case "it makes no sense to speak of events as *specially caused* by God" – or if there are special supernatural causes of specific events, God cannot be regarded as "in any sense the cause of regular events."[10] Thus, there is a very real peculiarity in the sort of overdetermination that appears to result from trying to maintain that a miracle is caused by God.

(c)   George Chryssides presents an ingenious argument according to which, if an event is a miracle, that is, a violation of a scientific law, then it cannot be attributed to an agent of any sort, divine or not; if it can be so attributed, then it is not a miracle. His reason is that "the assignment of agency implies predictability," the subsumption of the act under scientific law, yet this is impossible in the case of a miracle.[11] We assign agency when we have noted that similar actions by other agents in similar circumstances have been followed by similar subsequent events;[12] in the case of a miracle, however, we have a unique event to be assigned to a unique agent. Thus, once again, the question is raised as to how a miracle could possibly be connected with God.

But in spite of these sceptical views, there has not yet been a sufficiently radical questioning of the evidential connection between miracles and God. Odegard, for example, believes that an event identified as a miracle cannot be used as evidence for the existence of a god that is its cause. But his reason is that in order to say that the event is a miracle, we first have to say that it is caused by a god.[13] Similarly, Walker believes that "violation miracles" cannot "form the foundation of any sort of religious polemic," because "any polemic which endeavoured to demonstrate the existence of supernatural forces by means of the violation concept of the miraculous would have to assume the very existence of that which was the object of proof in order to maintain consistency in the proof itself."[14]

By contrast, I propose the suggestion that if a miracle in the sense used here were to occur, it would in fact constitute evidence *against* the existence of the Christian God. So, far from its being the case that identifying event x as a miracle would require one first to know that it is caused by God or a god, on the contrary, if one knew that God exists, then probably nothing could be identified as a miracle, and conversely, if event x could be identified as a miracle, one would have good reason to believe that God does not exist. Put simply, my view is that a miracle as an event that is a violation of natural law or that is permanently inexplicable is inconsistent with the concept of God.

I shall now try to give some defence of this suggestion. In so doing I shall perhaps be led into the quagmires of anthropomorphism, but perhaps this is inevitable in dealing with what seems to be an irretrievably anthropomorphic concept.

I propose, first, that we must ask some fundamental questions about the nature of a being that would cause miracles. Douglas K. Erlandson has suggested that the issue here is one of appropriateness: "the believer regards certain acts as appropriate to his God, other acts as inappropriate."[15] But to speak of "appropriateness" suggests, perhaps, a sort of cosmic politeness; so I think that a better word here would be "consistency." Are events that violate natural law or that are permanently inexplicable consistent with the nature of God?

In the past, some philosophers and theologians have urged us to consider the supposed order, regularity, and harmony of the universe as evidence of the existence of a benign and omnipotent god. But if order, regularity, and harmony constitute evidence for God, then miracles cannot *also* be accepted as evidence for his existence, for they are, to follow the metaphor, dissonances in the harmony, holes in the patterned fabric of the universe. Hence, a Christian believer cannot have it both ways. A miracle, a violation of natural law or a permanently inexplicable event, is a moment of chaos, a gap in the spatio-temporal structure. If one were to occur, it would therefore have to constitute evidence against the Christian God's existence.

It might, however, be objected that a miracle is not just a meaningless hole in nature's fabric, for after all, it is claimed to have a purpose, a function. As Erlandson remarks, "Inexplicability or mystery *is* an element of the miraculous, but it must be of a certain sort – it must fit a pattern"[16] – not, presumably, a pattern of natural events (for it disrupts them) – but an intelligible pattern of divine activity.

But then the focus of our interest must switch to a consideration of God's supposed purposes and intentions. As Herbert Burhenn remarks, questions about the attribution of miracles are "teleological rather than causal in character."[17] In particular, is a violation of law or an inexplicable event congruent with the purposes of a benevolent God?

I would suggest that it is not. For such an event is misleading to human beings who, as knowledge-seekers, attempt to understand the world by discerning the regularities and patterns in it. The extreme rarity of miracles and the difficulties and controversies in identifying them are an impediment to the growth of scientific and philosophical comprehension. A benevolent God would not mislead his people.

Two related answers to this argument are possible. First, it might be argued that the occurrence of a miracle does not, in fact, have this puzzling effect, because the event itself is part of a *pattern* of the miraculous. Thus, for the religious believer, two very general patterns are discernible: the pattern of natural events, which is studied by science, and the pattern of divine events, consisting of interventions in the natural order.[18] As Erlandson remarks, "the pattern that the believer perceives extends to many events. Rarely will the believer see only one event as miraculous. Rather, he can point to a series of events which he perceives to be acts of his God. This series presents an overall pattern to the believer, from which he can ascertain the nature of his God, and which provides him justification for deciding that a particular occurrence is a miracle."[19]

Unfortunately, one fact seems to militate against this response, and that is the rarity of miracles. It has a twofold implication. On the one hand, if miracles really do occur infrequently, as they seem to, it will be difficult to discern a pattern of meaning in their occurrence, and there will be controversy as to what the pattern is. On the other hand, if their occurrence were not so rare, then to that degree they would be more disruptive of human efforts to see the world as forming a coherent, unified, consistent pattern. Thus Erlandson is mistaken in supposing that "the believer can hold that some events are to be explained by appeal to the miraculous without in any way impugning scientific autonomy."[20] For, by its very nature, any alleged "pattern" of miraculous occurrences is inconsistent with the pattern of natural events which science seeks to account for, and there is very real epistemic dissonance between the two systems.

A second possible response to the claim that a benevolent God would not mislead his people by causing events that are a violation of natural law or are permanently inexplicable is the following. Some slight confusion in our growing understanding of the world is but a small price to pay for the other goods that a miracle would afford us. For example, "It might accomplish some positive good, such as healing or saving a life ... It might aid in the communication of divine teaching ... It might serve to revive religious awareness."[21]

But two important questions can be raised about such possible purposes. First, in being accomplished through miracles, they would seem to make use of human weaknesses – for example, fear, suggestibility, ignorance, and awe of the unknown. Second, and more important, this appeal to God's purposes creates an opening for some of the same moves that are made in the argument from evil against God's existence: "[O]ne could ask why an omnipotent God does not accomplish more and more good miraculously, or why he did not create a better world which would not require miraculous intervention to correct its faults."[22]

If accomplishing good, communicating divine teaching, or reviving religious awareness are divine purposes, miracles seem scarcely adequate to their accomplishment, for few people have been helped, and many remain sceptical. Certainly, if we consider the standard Biblical examples of miracles, they reflect a certain caprice – one is cured, another is not; bias – in favour of one group of people over another; and triviality. These events do not appear to be consistent with the sorts of purposes that might be supposed to be held by an omnipotent, omniscient, benevolent being. And even if one were not to use these events as standard examples of miracles, still, the very fact that a miracle is an event and therefore limited in space and time (albeit detached from the natural space-time continuum) means that it is inherently handicapped for conveying the purposes of a limitless God.

I conclude, then, that the reservations of philosophers such as Erlandson, McKinnon, and Chryssides about the connection between miracles and God are a step in the right direction but that they do not go far enough. For we must question the underlying assumption, ordinarily made by all parties to the debate, that if a miracle, in the sense of a violation of natural law or a permanently inexplicable event, were to occur, then it would be evidence for God's existence. On the contrary, if my arguments are correct, then if a miracle were to occur we would have a very good reason for denying that the Christian God exists. Paul Dietl claims that proving the existence of a being who deserves *some* of the predicates (for example, sufficient power to cause a violation of scientific law or a permanently inexplicable event) "God" normally gets would go some way toward proving the existence of God himself.[23] But if I am right, such a being, if it exists, could not have the characteristics we usually attribute to God and thus could not be the Christian God.

NOTES

My thanks are due to Keith Parsons, whose unpublished paper "Miracles" gave me the impetus to write this paper.

1 Herbert Burhenn, "Attributing Miracles to Agents – Reply to George D. Chryssides," *Religious Studies* 13 (1977): 485.
2 Cf. "[I]f we can establish that [an] event is produced by a god, the question of whether the event is a miracle may seem academic, since the ultimate goal is to find evidence of a god's existence ... The power to create miracles is often a central feature of a god, and if the given type of event is not a miracle, the defended god would be stripped of such power, which would be a large conceptual sacri-

fice." Douglas Odegard, "Miracles and Good Evidence," *Religious Studies* 18 (1982): 39.

3 John Hick, *Philosophy of Religion*, 3d. ed. (Englewood Cliffs, NJ: Prentice-Hall 1983), 14.

4 Odegard, "Miracles," 37; cf. 41.

5 Ian Walker, "Miracles and Violations," *International Journal for Philosophy of Religion* 13 (1982): 108.

6 David Basinger, "Miracles as Violations: Some Clarifications," *The Southern Journal of Philosophy* 22 (1984): 7, my emphasis.

7 However, Basinger denies that a nonrepeatable counterinstance to a law, caused by God, would be a violation of natural law, since it does not occur under the exact set of natural conditions presupposed in any set of natural laws (ibid., 5). But since my argument concerns whether a special event can be linked to God in any way, it seems safe for me to define a miracle as a violation of natural law. For my point is that we cannot start with a definition that assumes God's role in producing the event.

8 Douglas K. Erlandson, "A New Look at Miracles," *Religious Studies* 13 (1977): 421, his emphasis.

9 Alastair McKinnon, "'Miracle' and 'Paradox,'" *Analytical Philosophy of Religion in Canada*, ed. Mostafa Faghfoury (Ottawa: University of Ottawa Press 1982), p. 162.

10 Ibid., McKinnon's emphasis.

11 George D. Chryssides, "Miracles and Agents," *Religious Studies* 11 (1975): 322.

12 Ibid., 323–4.

13 Odegard, "Miracles," 45.

14 Walker, "Miracles and Violations," 108.

15 Erlandson, "A New Look at Miracles," 422. However, Erlandson gives what would seem by the standards of most believers to be a most inappropriate example: God's curing a hangnail in response to prayers by a man of faith!

16 Ibid., 423, his emphasis.

17 Burhenn, "Attributing Miracles," 489.

18 Cf. Erlandson, "A New Look at Miracles," 426.

19 Ibid., 424.

20 Ibid., 427.

21 Burhenn, "Attributing Miracles," 488.

22 Ibid.

23 Paul Dietl, "On Miracles," *American Philosophical Quarterly* 5 (1968): 133.

16 Miracles and the Existence of God: A Reply

ROBERT LARMER

In chapter 15, Christine Overall suggests that "there has been far too little attention paid to the alleged evidential connections between the existence of miracles and the existence of God." She goes on to develop the startling thesis that any event we might be prepared to call a miracle would be evidence *against* the existence of God. Rejecting the view that to call an event a miracle is, by definition, to say that God exists, she goes on to urge that if the theist believes that the regularity and harmony of the universe constitute evidence for God's existence, he can scarcely argue that miracles are also evidence for God's existence. Inasmuch as miracles are irregular events, they must be conceived as "moment[s] of chaos ... gap[s] in the spatio-temporal structure" of the universe. Thus, if God is conceived as a God of order and harmony, miracles constitute evidence not for His existence, but rather for His nonexistence.

Overall considers that if the divine purposes are to accomplish good, communicate divine teaching, or revive religious awareness, miracles can scarcely be adequate to their accomplishment, since "if we consider the standard Biblical examples of miracles, they reflect a certain caprice – one is cured, another is not; bias – in favour of one group of people over another; and triviality." She goes on to say that, even if we do not use the biblical accounts as standard examples, "the very fact that a miracle is an event, and therefore limited in space and time (albeit detached from the natural space-time continuum) means that it is inherently handicapped for conveying the purposes of a limitless God." Overall's argument, although she does not explicitly characterize it as such, seems basically a variation on the problem of evil. On her view, miracles constitute a cognitive evil: inasmuch as they prevent us from understanding the world, a good God could not allow them to occur. Any evidence, therefore, for the existence of the Judaeo-Christian God is evidence against miracles, and any evidence for miracles is evidence against the existence of such a God.

Philosophers differ on how serious a challenge the existence of evil poses to theism. Fortunately, however, there is no need to delve deeply into the problem of evil to rebut Overall's argument. Whether or not it has any force depends on whether miracles really constitute cognitive evils. If they do not, then her argument cannot even get started. What I propose to show is that she does not provide any good reasons for thinking miracles are cognitive evils.

Whether or not it is plausible to think of miracles as cognitive evils will depend very largely on how "miracle" is defined. It is significant, therefore, that Overall misdefines "miracle." She considers a miracle to be either a violation of the laws of nature or a permanently inexplicable event. Neither of these definitions is adequate.

Although it is very prevalent, the view that a miracle must violate the laws of nature is simply false. I have shown that miracles in the strong sense of events that nature would not produce on its own can occur in a world that behaves always and everywhere completely in accordance with the laws of nature.[1] The crux of my argument depends upon distinguishing between the laws of nature and the "stuff" of the material world whose behaviour they describe. Once this distinction has been made, we can see that it is logically possible for God, by the creation or annihilation of the "stuff" of the material world, to change the material conditions to which the laws of nature apply, without in any way violating the laws of nature. He would thereby produce an event that nature would not have produced on its own.

If my argument is correct, there is no need to import into the concept of miracle the cognitive difficulties and perplexities that so plague the violation model.

Overall's alternative definition does not fare any better. She follows David Basinger in suggesting that a miracle can be defined as a permanently inexplicable event. Unfortunately, Basinger is confused on this point. He takes the phrase "permanently inexplicable" to be equivalent to the phrase "not subsumable under natural law."[2] This, however, is to beg the question of what form an explanation may take. Miracles are usually conceived to be, in some sense, direct acts of God. Both in Scripture and more modern accounts they are explained by referring to the desires and purposes of a transcendent agent. What Swinburne has called "personal" explanation, that is, explanation in terms of agency, is a concept essential to the notion of the miraculous, and provided it can be defended, there is no reason to define miracles as permanently inexplicable events. Indeed, to attempt to do so is to betray a misunderstanding of how the term is actually used. Those who believe in miracles do not think of them as permanently inexplicable events but rather as events that especially reveal the character and purposes of God.

Overall might be tempted to reply that my criticisms of the definitions she proposes miss the point entirely. She might claim that what is at issue is whether certain special and unusual events can be linked to God. We cannot begin, therefore, with a definition that assumes God's role in producing the event.

Tempting though it might be, such a reply cannot prove successful. By way of seeing why, let us distinguish two questions: (1) What is a miracle? and (2) What events are properly called miracles? Note that the first question concerns the intension of the term, whereas the second question concerns the extension of the term. Note also that extension is determined by intension.[3] Put somewhat differently, before we can answer the question, What events are properly called miracles? we must first answer the question, What is a miracle? In her discussion, Overall has the problem backwards. She assumes that we can readily identify miracles as a class and that our problem is one of abstracting a definition so as to arrive at the term's intensional meaning. She then proceeds to redefine the term "miracle," arriving in the process at a definition that has little resemblance to the way the term is actually used.⁴

It is only by misdefining miracle that Overall is able to claim that if miracles occur, they frustrate any attempt to understand the world. Only if we accept her insistence that a miracle must violate the laws of nature or that it is a permanently inexplicable event does it follow that a miracle is an impediment to the growth of scientific and philosophical comprehension. To call an event a miracle *is* to explain it; it is to explain it in terms of God's purposes and desires. The believer who calls a particular event a miracle is not simply noting that it is unusual or unexpected but making a claim about its cause. If a miracle occurs and we recognize it to be such, we understand the world better, since we are correctly identifying its causal antecedents.

Neither will it do for her merely to assert that "by its very nature, any alleged 'pattern' of miraculous occurrences is inconsistent with the pattern of natural events that science seeks to account for." The demand that all reality be interrelated and consistent is legitimate. However, in insisting that any alleged pattern of miraculous occurrences cannot be consistent with the pattern of natural events, Overall begs the question of whether nature constitutes the whole of reality or is only a partial system within it, thereby begging the question of whether miracles constitute a cognitive evil. Unless we presuppose the falsity of theism, the epistemic dissonance she speaks of is more apparent than real. It seems quite possible for the theist to relate these two patterns. As C.S. Lewis notes,

In the forward direction (i.e. during the time which follows its occurrence) it [a miracle] is interlocked with all Nature just like any other event. Its peculiarity is that it is not in that way interlocked backwards, interlocked with the previous history of Nature ... the miracle and the previous history of Nature may be interlocked ... but not in the way the Naturalist expected: rather in a much more roundabout fashion. The great complex event called Nature, and the new particular event introduced into it by the miracle, are related by their common origin in God, and doubtless, if we knew enough, most intricately related in His purpose and design, so that a Nature which had had a different history, and therefore been a different Nature, would have been invaded by different miracles or by none at all. In that way the miracle and the previous course of Nature are as well interlocked as any other two realities, but you must go back as far as their common Creator to find the interlocking. You will not find it within Nature ... Everything is connected with everything else: but not all things are connected by the short and straight roads we expected.[5]

Similarly, it will not do for Overall simply to assert that the standard biblical examples of miracles reflect a certain caprice, bias, and triviality. Millions of people who have read these texts seriously find exactly the opposite. John Henry Newman, for example, argued that the miracles that cannot easily be seen to have religious significance "are but a few in the midst of an overpowering majority consistently pointing to one grand object; they must not be torn from their moral context, but, on the credit of the rest, they must be considered but apparent exceptions ... It is obvious that a large system must consist of various parts of unequal utility and excellence; and to expect each particular occurrence to be complete in itself is as unreasonable as to require the parts of some complicated machine, separately taken, to be all equally finished and fit for display."[6] Until she comes to grips with arguments such as Newman's and until she provides some positive argument for her assertion that the standard biblical examples of miracle reflect caprice, bias, and triviality, Overall's claim is question-begging.

Finally, Overall's claim that because a miracle is an event and therefore limited in space and time, it is inherently inadequate for conveying the purposes of God is suspect. How is God to convey His purposes to spatio-temporal creatures except through events of some sort? How can God convey His purposes to a particular person at a particular place at a particular time except through a particular event or series of events? Certainly prayer, no less than miracles, presupposes a spatio-temporal setting, since if God conveys His purposes to a person in prayer, He must do so at a particular time and place. If God can convey His purposes through one, there seems no reason to think He cannot convey His purposes through the other.

Overall cannot claim that miracles are an inadequate vehicle for conveying God's purposes unless she is also prepared to argue that it is logically impossible that God can communicate with spatio-temporal creatures at all. She has given no indication that she wants to claim this and, more importantly, has given no argument capable of supporting such a claim. Her assertion that a miracle cannot convey the purposes of God remains unsupported, as does her assertion that miracles constitute evidence against God's existence.

NOTES

1 See this volume, chapter 3, and Robert Larmer, *Water Into Wine?* (Montreal: McGill-Queen's University Press 1988).
2 David Basinger, "Miracles As Violations: Some Clarifications," *The Southern Journal of Philosophy* 22 (1984): 6.
3 Irving M. Copi, *Introduction to Logic*, 6th ed. (New York: Macmillan 1982), 156–7.
4 Overall might be tempted to protest that I have been unduly harsh. I do not think I have. Granted that the idea that a miracle involves a violation of a law of nature is a time-honoured one, to attempt to define a miracle solely as a violation of a law of nature is to stray very far from how the term is actually used. At most, and I would deny that it even does this, the idea that a miracle involves a violation of a law of nature expresses a necessary condition of an event being a miracle, not a sufficient condition. Similarly in the case of defining a miracle as an inexplicable event. Neither definition does justice to the richness of the term.
5 C.S. Lewis, *Miracles: A Preliminary Study.* (London: The Centary Press 1947), 73–4.
6 John Henry Newman, *Two Essays on Biblical and on Ecclesiastical Miracles* (London: Longmans, Green 1890), 47.

Contributors

DAVID BASINGER teaches in the Division of Religion and Humanities at Roberts Wesleyan College in Rochester, New York. His area of special interest is philosophy of religion.

JOHN COLLIER teaches in the Department of Philosophy at the University of Newcastle in Callaghan, New South Wales, Australia. His area of special interest is philosophy of science.

ROBERT LARMER teaches in the Department of Philosophy at the University of New Brunswick in Fredericton, New Brunswick. His area of special interest is philosophy of religion.

NEIL MacGILL teaches in the Department of Philosophy at the University of New Brunswick in Fredericton, New Brunswick. His areas of special interest are ethics and linguistic philosophy.

CHRISTINE OVERALL teaches in the Department of Philosophy at Queen's University in Kingston, Ontario. Her areas of special interest are feminism and epistemology.

PHILLIP WIEBE teaches in the Department of Philosophy at Trinity Western University in Langley, British Columbia. His areas of special interest are philosophy of science and epistemology.

FRED WILSON teaches in the Department of Philosophy at the University of Toronto. His areas of special interest are philosophy of science and the history of philosophy.

Index

Shaftesbury, A., 5,
  17n8
Sherlock, T., xxi
Sherwin-White, A.N.,
  102
Spinoza, B., xv, xvi,
  xvii, xxi
Strauss, D., xxii

suffering, xiii
Swinburne, R., 89, 90

testimony, xiii, xix, xx,
  xxiii, 4, 5, 9–15,
  27–9, 31, 33–5, 57
theoretical entities, 63,
  70

Tillotson, J., 10
Troeltsch, E., xxii,
  xxiii

Wiebe, P., 121–31
Wilkins, J., xvii
Wilson, F., 26–8, 31–2
Wollaston, W., xxi